Alusru:

Her Tears Became Pearls

Ursula Tillberg Robinson

A publication of

Eber & Wein Publishing

Pennsylvania

Alusru: Her Tears Became Pearls

Library of Congress
Cataloging in Publication Data

ISBN 978-1-60880-616-4

Proudly manufactured in the United States of America by

Eber & Wein Publishing

Pennsylvania

First of all, I'd like to dedicate this book to all who believed in me and also to those who didn't.

I'd like to express my gratitude to my friends and family, but especially Opa and his deep love for Jesus. He always closed his prayers with the words, "Lord, not my will, but Your will be done!"

I'd also like to express my special gratitude to Reverend Billy Graham and Pastor Benny Hinn. Reverend Billy Graham came to Germany and planted the desire in my heart to come to America. Pastor Benny Hinn made it possible for me to fulfill my deepest unspoken wish to walk where Jesus walked—to visit Jerusalem and the Holy Land and spend ten days in Israel.

I thank the Lord for all my children: Pamela and Troy, Michael, Christian, Daniel and Trista, my grandchildren, Katie and Jacob, Jessie and Kyle, and Manny, Jacob, and Ariel, and my great-granddaughter Karrah. Thank You, Lord, for Dennis—my husband of twenty-six years and the father of my children. Thank You, Lord, for my husband Jerry—father to of my wonderful new daughter Brenda and her husband Chris, and grandfather to my very special grandson Aaron.

The Lord also gave me special friends who helped me: Don and Cheri, Jo Ann, Lorraine, and many more. Thank you to Rachel Barduson who helped me to write the book and to Chandler and Eber & Wein for all the help.

To everyone who reads my book, thank you and remember God is closer than you think, and He answers our prayers!

A special thank you goes to my granddaughter Jessie. She designed and drew the picture for the cover and brought back my dream. Jessie was born in Panama, grew up in Minnesota, and she and Kyle are proud and happy parents of daughter Karrah Rhianna, who will soon be two years. Thank you, Jessie! I know Jesus loves you! Keep your eyes on Jesus and He will never leave you!

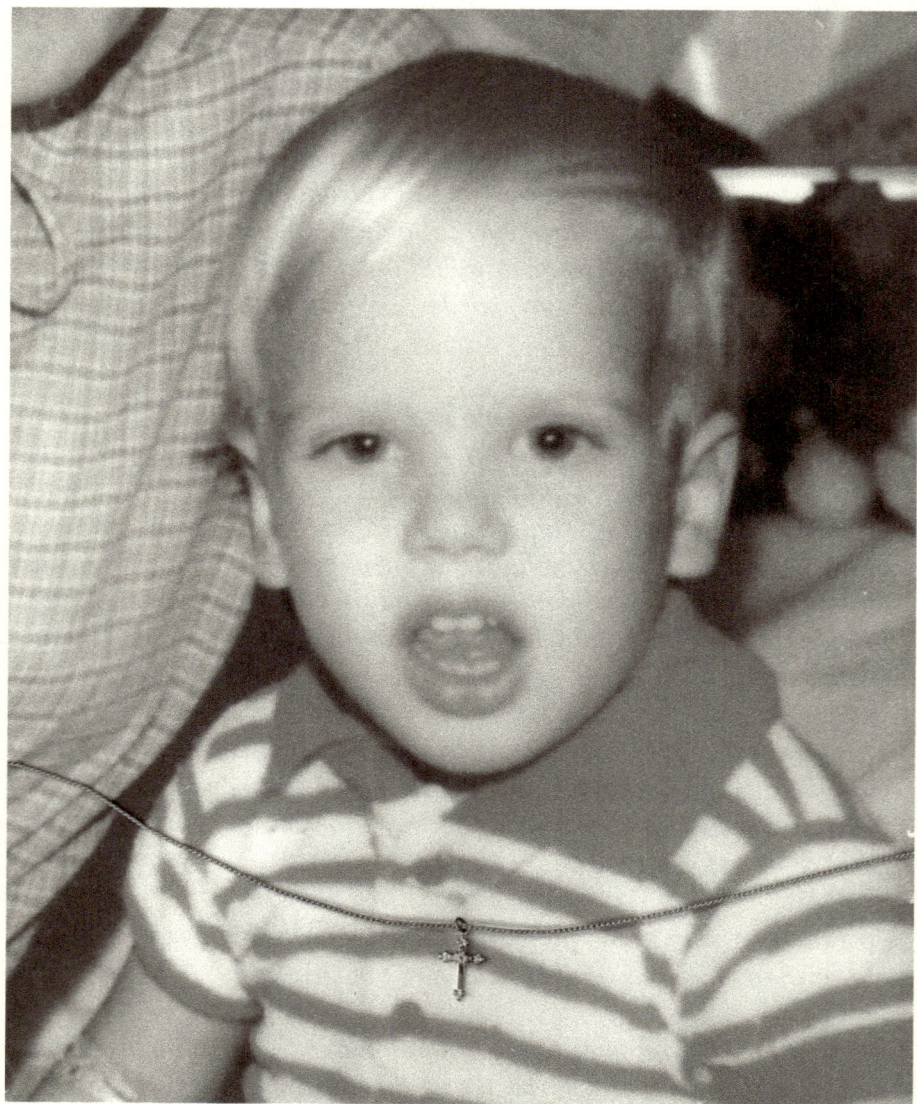

Contents

Preface

As the writer of this story, it is, more or less, a true story of my life and that of my family. It is a testimony of faith and trust in the Lord. To this day, I still say that without the Lord and His unconditional love I would not be here; whatever I did and accomplished in my life was only because of prayers and God's answers. The glory and honor belongs to God alone.

I shared many things with my friends and family and decided to write everything down. If I had a chance, I might use all my words and memories to publish a book and pass it on to generations to come. It took me a long time to start over again; I had written over two hundred pages about twenty years ago. We moved, and I lost everything except for some of my mother's and my original notes, which were a reminder to write my life story and pass it on to my family—my children and grandchildren—and friends.

First of all, I think I should acquaint my reader with the country where I was born. My homeland is Germany. I grew up in Westphalia, which is located in the central part of West Germany. West Germany is approximately the size of the state of California. I was born in Bochum—the city had about as many people as Minneapolis in Minnesota.

After World War II, Germany was divided into East and West Germany. West Germany was led by a democratic government, and East Germany was controlled by a communistic regime. It was a very difficult time for the people in Germany. East Germany was separated from West Germany through a huge wall, and it was impossible to have contact with people living on the west side. The wall was built August 12, 1961—over night. People who were on the east side were unable to get to their families on the west side. It was unbelievable how the wall was built; it went through homes and buildings. It separated many children from their parents. If they were on the east side at the time the wall was built, they were unable to get back to their home on the west side to their parents and friends.

Indeed, the Berlin Wall was a shock to the world. Anyone who tried to climb or break the wall was killed. I don't know how many people lost their lives. I still remember when a group of people got together and tried to dig a tunnel under the wall to free ten children and bring them back to their families. It was just before Christmas, and after the children were brought back, every one of their helpers was caught and killed.

When President Ronald Reagan visited Berlin, he told Mikhail Gorbachew to tear the wall down. After more than twenty-seven years, the wall was finally taken down. On November 9, 1989, Mikhail Gorbachew gave the order to tear down the wall, and the whole world was relieved and celebrated that day.

I will tell more about my homeland. After the war, Germany had to rebuild, because the country was in ashes. Only the little villages are still the same today; they never lost their beauty. Germany is a beautiful country, and if you decide to visit Germany you might agree with me. Germany has mountains with everlasting snow and ice. It has big cities and large flatland with deep, blue sees and beautiful lakes and castles. The Rhine, the Danube, and the Elbe are the most famous rivers. A trip on a riverboat will bring the visitor to wonderful castles and old churches. If I have to give a short description, I put it in this way: Germany has all the beauty concentrated in a small place. In the southern part of Germany you will find a small island where people grow tropical fruit and flowers, because it is close to the Gulf of Mexico and the climate is more tropical.

The climate of Germany can be compared with the climate in Minnesota—perhaps not as cold, but basically the same. Heavy rain and wind is also common in Germany, but before I came to the United

States I didn't know what a tornado or a hurricane was. I also had no idea what a mosquito was. I learned many things about America when I went to school in Germany, and I never thought that I ever would be able to see this great country. When I came for a visit, I never believed years later I would come back to live in the land of my dream—in the land of endless opportunities, in the land of the free!

1

The Miracle Letter, Birth of My Mom

The people in Germany are hard workers and take a firm stand in their beliefs, religion, and feelings. When I went to school, I had to walk about five miles, and we had school six days a week. No school bus, no school lunch. It was important to get a good education and to learn the basics, which were handwriting, math, reading, and grammar. We never had the opportunity to learn to drive or get a driving permit. We could not do training during our school time. School was all year, six days a week, with only four weeks summer vacation and a few days off on Easter and Christmas.

When I look back, I still remember when we all celebrated every morning before Christmas, and we had candles on our desk and evergreen branches. We sang and the teacher read a story because it was only four weeks until we would sing "Silent Night." This four weeks were the Advent season, and during this time we made decorations for the Christmas tree, shared special stories, and brought cookies to munch and hot coco to drink. I never wanted to miss Advent because it was special and brought us all closer to the Lord.

Germany had very strict rules and regulations regarding food and the health of children. If the word *kinder* was used, sugar, salt, and additives—like preservatives and food color—were not allowed in any food specified for babies and children. We had also many places where people could buy only meat (*metzgerei*). Other stores had only bread and cake items (*baeckery*). The bakeries baked their own bread, cookies, and cakes with their own secret recipes. When you passed by a bakery, you could smell the yeast and fresh-baked bread.

Fruit and vegetables were not imported; they were grown in Germany. Many bread stores delivered fresh-baked rolls and Danish early in the morning. The milkman also brought fresh milk to the homes in the morning. He rang a big bell and everyone came and got fresh milk direct from the farm.

My mom made butter, cheese, and cream. It was a special treat for us when she had sour milk for dessert with cinnamon and sugar. Mom was always busy; she made most of my dresses. She sewed, knit, and crocheted.

Mom and Dad made the rules, and we had to follow them or face the consequences. We were raised with love and discipline. My dad worked on the railroad and was also a sports teacher and coach. He was very busy, and sometimes he was gone two or three days. When Dad took us on the train, it was always a special treat, and I enjoyed very much listening to the whistle and looking out the window, watching the heavy steam go by. I thought it was great and so much fun. I enjoyed riding on a train pulled by a huge steaming, black locomotive or engine and listening to the shrill noise of the breaks when the train stopped or slowed down. My dad was in charge of all the bags, suitcases, boxes, and cages. Sometimes he had cages with dogs or cats, and he needed to be very careful, but my dad always had a special treat for them.

I will also tell you things I still remember from when I was very young. My dad was not home because he had to fight under the order from Adolf Hitler, and my mom was worried about him. I remember she often sat at the table and cried, but I also never forgot her answer when we asked why she was crying. She became very stern, looked at us and told us that she was not crying, and God let moms have tears when they were not able to go to the bathroom. Well, that was her answer.

My mom tried to keep all bad things away from us. Her stepdad was living with us, and he was the best grandpa to us kids. He was a police officer and helped many people because he loved the Lord. Grandpa (*Opa* in German) told me all the time that Jesus loves me, even when I was naughty. Indeed, Opa was the most important person in my life. He took care of my grandma with two little children. My mom was not very interested in going to school every day, but her brother was a genius; he had no problems learning, and nothing was difficult for him. When he was a young man, he could speak several different languages. He became a pastor and a director in the mission field.

My mom and her brother didn't have a close relationship with each other. My uncle was not very pleased that Mom was his only sister. When we decided to visit him, we had to make an appointment. I remember one time when we went to Bochum to see my mom's cousin. I begged mom to see Aunt Hanna and Uncle Albert. Mom didn't like the idea but finally gave in, and we went to visit without making an appointment.

My uncle was not very nice to Mom because he had a very important visitor—the bishop from his church. When we entered the room the bishop looked at my mom and ask my uncle who she was. My uncle said, "Mrs. Leitsnen, and this is her daughter."

I was not very happy. I looked at my uncle and shouted, "My name is Alusru, and this is my mom; she is Uncle Albert's sister, and I am his niece. We came to visit."

The bishop was a very nice person and smiled at me. Then he looked at my uncle and said, "Albert, you never told me that you have a sister, but I am very pleased to meet her and also your sweet little niece."

I could see my uncle was not very happy to see us, and all he said was sorry, but I never talk about my family. I had the feeling that my uncle lived in another world—a world in which we didn't have any place.

So I will skip this chapter and move on to tell more about things I remember when I still was very little and we lived in Bochum. Opa came home from work. Mom had given us a bath, and I was playing with my dolls. It was very quiet, but then everything changed, and the sound of many sirens called the attention of the people. Opa took my brother, and Mom tried to grab me, but I refused and told her that I wanted to play. The sirens started again very loudly. Opa took my hand and said, "I will play with you after we come back, but now we have to go."

I finally took my dolls and put them in my bed. Then I followed Mom, Opa, and my brother. We went to a bunker across the street, and I began to cry because I wanted my dolls. Opa went back to the house and came back just in time before the bunker was closed. He gave me my dolls and a little blanket. He also gave my brother his teddy bear.

A man was standing by the door, and he was a soldier. He looked at his watch and told us that we could leave in about forty-five minutes. I will never forget the terrible noises, the shaking, the banging, and the screaming. To this day, I am very much afraid of thunder and lightning, and do not enjoy watching fireworks.

After the noise stopped, we could leave but not to our homes because there were no homes anymore—no stores, no factories, no bridges, no trees, no churches, no streets—nothing! Everything was gone. Bochum was burning and totally gone. I will never forget the smell, and I still remember the big holes all over and the lady with a red cross on her shirt; she put a wet cloth over my mouth and gave us some water to drink.

I remember that I cried when a young girl was walking on the other side of the street and there was loud screaming and fire, and then she was gone. I was so afraid and was holding onto Mom. What had happened? Where was the girl? I remember that Mom told me not to look to the other side. It was good that I didn't look, because I found out later that the girl had stepped on a mine and it exploded. Opa had to leave and help other people.

We went to stay with some relatives out in the country. We were all loaded on a big truck and brought to the country. Then we had to walk a long way to a small village. It was Sunday, and when we arrived, people had just left the church service. They were all dressed in nice clothes; we were dirty, tired, and hungry. I remember the man who talked to Mom; he was not very nice and got angry because he didn't like children and didn't wanted us to stay at his house, even though he was the richest farmer in the village. He did not like to let anyone stay unless they worked for him. Mom told him that she had no place to go and that she would work for him. He finally let us stay but only in the barn section and only for a short time.

I will not write very much about this time. I will now stop and tell more about my mom, my grandma and Mom's dad.

My mom was born in 1914 during World War I. She and her brother had to grow up without a dad until Grandma married Opa, who very much loved children and took care of every need.

Mom told me many things about her mom and the time Grandma was waiting for an answer from her husband; he was fighting for the country in Siberia, and the last word came from the swamp in Masuria in Russia. It was June 28, 1914. Two shots fired by a student from Serbia had killed the Archduke and his wife from Austria/Hungary. Serbia was an enemy to Austria and was protected by Russia. The assassination caused Austria and Hungary to declare War on Serbia a month later. A chain reaction followed through Europe with Russia, Germany, and Britain. Russia fought for Serbia and Germany fought Russia. So the result was that Britain declared war on Germany.

In 1917, the United States of America became involved, and November 11, 1918, Germany surrendered. The Treaty of Versailles, signed June 28, 1919, punished Germany and became part of the reason for World War II. After the end of World War I, the world wanted to forget the war time and go back to normal, but political scandal and corruption brought the world to financial disaster. People tried to make easy money at the stock market. They bought stocks and borrowed money. October 24, 1929, the stock market crashed; it was called Black Thursday and the worst depression in history was underway.

I have told you in short something about the reason that the world fought two world wars, but I still do not believe that a war can help a country. I think the first reason is to gain more power, and to reach this the people in power will use corruption and lies, and they will kill anyone who stands in their way.

Later I will tell you more about World War II, but now I will go back to tell you about my grandma and my grandpa KK and God's will for both of them.

The year was 1914, and the word *war* was in every conversation. The people in cities and villages didn't know what to think about this short little word. When they tried to look it up in the dictionary, it didn't sound important and the meaning was simple: *armed conflict, as between two nations or countries.* But the reality was terrible, and all the young men were ordered to fight. They had no choice; some had no time to say goodbye to their families and loved ones. This word, *war* (*krieg*), brought tears and pain to the world. My grandpa (Mom's daddy) also had to leave. He would rather give anything to stay with his beautiful wife and his son Albert, but he had to go and didn't have much time to make any important arrangements for his family, so he was glad that Anna went home to stay with her parents. He knew they would take care of his wife and son. His wife was pregnant, and the time was very close that the baby would be born. Kaspar folded his hands and prayed to God to take care of everything.

In a little village in the east part of Germany, my grandma, Anna Elisabeth, who was living with her parents and was ready to give birth to her third child, decided to stay with her mom and dad until after her baby was born. Because her youngest brother was not very nice, he complained all the time that the farm was not bringing enough to feed two extra mouths. Wilhelm, her dad, was not very happy and had many problems with his son. He didn't like that he was so greedy and continuously mean to everyone, often yelling at the help.

The harvest was over and it was a very good year, but the farm had not enough help because, even though he paid very well, the help would not stay very long because of his son's hardhearted behavior.

Wilhelm watched his son very closely and would not allow him to be mean to his sister. He was glad he didn't give in to his son and sign the farm over to him. So he was still in charge of the farm, and he told his son that he would not allow him to treat his sister with disrespect.

Wilhelm decided to check on his daughter, and he went upstairs to her room. Liesel, his wife, was with Anna and tried to comfort her daughter when Heinrich entered the room. Anna was holding her little son Albert. She smiled when her dad entered the room. For the last hour she had started to have some contractions, and she could feel that her baby was ready to enter this world soon.

Her mom gave her a hug and said, "Maybe you take some rest and we should let you sleep for a while. I will take care of Albert and will check on you from time to time."

Anna agreed, and before she went to lie down, she gave her little son a kiss. She gave a hug to her parents and whispered, "Thank you, Mom and Dad; I love you both so much, but I wish Kaspar would be with me."

Anna tried to sleep but the contractions and the worries about her husband kept her from a good sleep. She was very much concerned about Kaspar. His last letter came about a month ago, and since that time she had no idea where he was.

The door opened and Liesel came to check on her daughter. She could see that it was time to call Babette the midwife, and so she left and told her husband to get ready for the birth.

Wilhelm gave a quick order to get the horse carriage ready and to drive to the village and pick up the midwife. He was very worried, and deep in his heart he prayed to God for help.

For the last two hours the contractions came very regularly and Liesel tried to comfort her daughter. She held her child's small, soft hand and told her that she would soon be holding a beautiful baby in her arms. Liesel wished to find a way to take the pain away from her child, but all she could do was hold her hand and tell her that she loved her. She saw that Anna's face was red and sweaty, so she took a cold cloth and wiped her face and forehead. Anna looked at her mother and said, "Mother, can you tell me why a woman has to go to so much pain to have a baby?"

Her mother looked at her child, smiled and answered, "You see, my child, this is what God wanted. The pain of having a child and becoming a mother will always be remembered by a mother. A mother will do anything to help and protect her child. You love your little boy, and you will also love your new baby."

All of sudden the door opened and Liesel saw her son. He was very angry and shouted at his mother, "You don't need to help because you don't need to be with her," (pointing at Anna, his sister). "Old Babette is here, and she gets paid to deliver. I need all the help on the farm, and the maid is not doing a good job so you need to come."

Liesel looked at her son, stood up, pointed her hand at the door and said very sternly, "Heinrich, close the door and send Babette up, and don't you ever tell me what to do. I can stop your dad from signing the farm over to you. I am still in charge of this place, and I think you need to remember this. Now leave and don't you slam the door."

Wilhelm came and with him the old Babette. Heinrich had no time to say anything, and so he grinded his teeth and left angry and furious. The old Babette smiled at Anna and said, "Well, sometimes I wish that men like your brother would have contractions and give birth, but I think if this would be, the world would soon not have any more babies. Well, Anna, let's see if your little boy is ready to be born. I think that is what you wish for, isn't it?"

Anna was not able to talk because she felt the baby was ready to come, but when the midwife said that she would have a boy, she began to cry and said, "I really hoped I would have a girl because KK—you see, I call my husband KK (King Kaspar)—and I would like to have a little girl."

Babette smiled, looked at Anna and said, "Well, my dear, what can we do if God has decided to bless you with another boy? I can only deliver with no return guarantee, and very soon we will see what God has given you. I think it is time to push. You see, God knows what is best for all of us."

Babette controlled everything and helped Anna to relax after each contraction. The old midwife knew how difficult it was when Dad wanted a boy and Mom gave birth to a girl. Often he was angry at his wife and didn't want to see the baby, but most of the time the midwife had a good conversation with the father, and when he held the little girl he was happy.

Anna now had a very heavy contraction and Babette said, "A few more pushes, and I can see your baby's blond hair; everything is fine and the baby has a good heartbeat."

Now it was time to give birth to her child (my mom). It was September 19, 1914, at 17:35 (5:35 PM) that she was born. Babette told Anna she had a beautiful girl, blue eyes and blond hair, almost eight pounds. Anna (my grandma), was happy, but deep in her heart she was sad; she wished her husband, Kaspar, would be here with her. She missed him very much, but she also had the feeling that she would never see him again, and that he never would hold his beautiful girl he had wished for when he found out Anna was pregnant.

Anna kissed her baby, wiped away the tears, and whispered, "Oh Kaspar, you have a beautiful daughter, and she needs to meet her wonderful daddy. Please, honey, come home. I miss you and love you so much."

Babette took care of Grandma and the screaming little new baby girl. She smiled, and after she was done cleaning up, she said, "You see, my dear, God granted your wish and also heard Kaspar's wish! Now you have a boy and a girl, and if you decide to have more children then it doesn't matter what it is, you will always love your child. Now you need some rest, and I will check on you tomorrow."

The midwife left.

Liesel was proud of her daughter. She held her new granddaughter in her arms and said, "Your daddy will be so happy, and you will see you have a great daddy. He will love you very much."

The baby smiled and sucked on her little finger. Wilhelm came and looked at his new grandchild and smiled at his daughter. He said, "She is a little princess, and I think Kaspar will be very proud of his daughter. Soon the war will be over, and he will be home. I am very proud of you, my daughter. Everything will be okay, and Kaspar will be home, but now you need to rest. I will make sure that your brother stays away from you, and Mother is watching princess. By the way, what name did you pick for this little sweetheart?"

Anna said, "KK likes the name Margret, and I think we will call her Anna Margret."

Wilhelm thought this was a nice name. He kissed his daughter, and soon Anna fell asleep. She was exhausted, and even though she couldn't stop thinking about Kaspar, the sleep took over. Her last thoughts were of Kaspar. She smiled. She dreamed about the time she met Kaspar, and her dream brought her back to the first dance. He called her a queen, and she called him a king. They danced all night and fell in love. He was good looking and showered her with flowers and gifts. He was a bricklayer and told her that he would build a house all by himself and she would help him to design every room. When Kaspar asked her to be his wife, she didn't hesitate and said *yes*. They had a wonderful wedding, and when she gave birth two years later to her first child Albert, they moved into the new home Kaspar had built. She was so happy.

A year later her second child was born, but he died after only twenty-four hours. My grandma was heartbroken and didn't want any more children. Her little boy was almost five when she found out that she was expecting another child. Kaspar was very happy, and he told her over and over again that everything is in God's hand and no one can do things better. God is in charge and we only have to trust and love Him. He took her in his arms and both danced. KK loved to dance, and Anna thought when he came home they could dance again—this time he would dance also with his little princess Margret.

Grandpa never came home, but four years later Grandma received a letter from Grandpa. When the military officer stopped at the house, Anna knew that it was bad or good news because she would hear something about Kaspar. The officer gave her a letter and said it was addressed to her. Anna recognized Kaspar's handwriting. Anna began to cry and held the letter close to her heart. She picked up her little girl Anna Margret. Her boy Albert came and put his little hand up reaching for the letter. He asked, "Is Daddy coming home, Mommy? Why are you crying?"

Anna thought to herself, I need to be strong. She wiped away her tears and slowly unfolded the letter. She began to read...

Again and again, I think my grandma was a great mother and tried to be strong. She loved the Lord and trusted Him all the time—that God was guiding her life and gave her comfort and love with this miracle letter.

My mom had this letter and read it many times to me. I can't remember how often I cried when I touched the letter. I wished I still would have the letter. I called it a miracle letter because Grandpa wrote it the exact same day and time when my mom was born.

When I came to the United States of America, I lost three of my suitcases with important papers and precious things, including the letter and many pictures. It got lost by the airline, but I will try to remember the letter and its details.

Date: September 19, 1914.   Time: 17:35 (5:35 PM)

My dear Anna!

Today is the last day that I can write to you and can tell you how much I love you and miss you and our little son. But most of all how much I miss to kiss and hold our little baby girl. I know that you right now gave birth to our beautiful girl Margret. Take good care of her and tell her every day that her daddy loves her very much. The commander told us to write home today because tomorrow we will have to fight and might not be able to have any more chances to write. I pray that you will receive this letter and that you know how much I love you and our children. You will always be my dream queen and Margret is my dream princess. I will put three kisses in this letter: the first is for you, my queen; the second is for our little soldier son, Albert; and the last kiss is for our sweet little princess, Margret. I know in my heart I will hold you in my arms if not on this earth, then it will be in Heaven. I love you and I pray that God will be on your side. Anna, my dear queen, you need to promise me that if I can't come home, please marry a good man who will love you and be a good father to our children. Keep your eyes on the Lord, He will watch over you and guide you. He let me see our little girl, and I know she has blue eyes and will have blond hair.

Remember, I will always be close to you and talk to you in your dreams. We will dance in your dreams. I love you.

LOVE,
KK—KING KASPAR

My grandpa loved the Lord, and I think God gave him the strength and the words to write this letter. God also made it possible that Grandma would receive the letter. When Grandma asked the battalion chief why it took so long for the letter to be delivered, the chief told her it was a wonder that the letter was found. One soldier from another group brought the letter home after he found it in a mailbag under snow in Russia. Only a few letters reached their destination. Indeed, it was a miracle and the beginning of a great journey with the Lord watching and guiding our family. I only can say: *If God is for us, who can be against us?* (Romans 8:31) With God, *all* things are *possible*! I can say that we sometimes have no answers, and we try to find an explanation for things rather than ask the Lord. It is so easy to reach out to God and let Him be in charge of everything—simple to give it *all* to Jesus Christ.

God had also brought another good man into Grandma's life. Opa loved children, but never had a child of his own because, during World War I, he was wounded and unable to father a child. He was told that he would get married and be a father to two children. At first he did not believe that he would ever get married and be a papa to two children, but when he saw Grandma he fell in love with her and remembered God's answer and prediction. He asked Grandma if she had children, and Grandma told him about Margret and Albert. Opa knew she was the one he had to marry. He was married to her till death made him a widower. He loved Grandma very much and spoiled the kids.

Grandma was only forty-six when she went home to be with the Lord and to dance with her king KK. Opa never got married again and took care of everything. He became Opa to more than two hundred needy children! Any child who came and knocked on his window could count on Opa, and his door was never closed. He also had a wonderful way to teach everyone about the Lord, and he was thankful he found my grandma.

My mom told me so much about Grandma and how much she loved the Lord. She prayed every day. Grandma was not very healthy, and most people really didn't know how sick she was. Grandma tried to ignore the shortness of breath and the permanent pain she suffered daily. Opa tried to do his best to take care of all the business. He was a police officer but was also taking care of a laundry business with a small candy store.

Mom told me that she loved to help Papa and put big table cloths from restaurants in a huge mangle. Albert helped in the candy store and always studied whenever he had time. Opa was worried about Grandma's health and did everything to help her and to put a beautiful smile on her face, surprising her with a special gift or a bouquet of red roses or purple violets.

Grandma's heart was very weak, and she had a difficult time doing things she wanted to do. She never complained or got upset, but she needed to be admitted to the hospital many times. When Opa married Grandma, my mom was just six years old, and since she didn't know her real daddy, Opa was her Papa. He wanted to secure the future of the children and give them the land and properties he had, but he was not allowed to do this; he needed to sell all his land and open a bank account for the children. Money and security was more important. No one believed that the whole world would soon have to face a big inflation and another world war.

Today, I think that Grandma was worried about her children, especially her daughter, my mom. When she met my dad, Grandma did everything in her power to make him marry my mom. Mom was not ready to get married. She fell in love with my dad but wanted to wait a few more years to get married. She finally gave in and married my dad when she just turned twenty. I think Grandma pushed my mom to get married because Opa was not her father; he was her very young stepfather, and by the existing law, he would not be able to live with Mom in the same home.

Mom and Dad got married. She had a beautiful wedding, and Opa made sure that she also had enough of everything—including a wonderful honeymoon. My mom told me many times that she wished she wouldn't have gone on her honeymoon because when she said goodbye to her mom, she didn't know that it would be goodbye forever.

Grandma had another heart attack and was rushed to the hospital. It was a Sunday morning, and Opa was ready to leave. The professor came and told him they would get together and decide what could be done to help Grandma. He thought since she was very young there was a good chance to do treatment and to find some answers to help her.

The next morning, about ten doctors came to see my grandma. Everyone listened to her heart and agreed that they would be able to get her some relief. Grandma smiled and said that she was ready to go home. She turned her head, took a deep breath, and whispered, "Yes, I am ready to come home, KK, and dance with you."

A young student looked at her and shouted, "Oh my God, this lady is dead!"

The professor and the whole staff could not believe that Grandma was gone. No one believed that she just closed her eyes, turned her head, smiled, and died so peacefully.

Opa had promised Grandma that he would take care of everything and thanked her over and over for the great time he had with her. I know he loved Grandma very much and missed her every day. He gave the laundry business to Mom and Dad and sold the candy store and gave the money to Uncle Albert. He worked as a police officer and helped many people, especially children.

My dad was the oldest son in his family, having three sisters and two brothers. His mom was very angry when Dad married my mom. She never tried to accept Mom as a daughter-in-law. In her eyes, Mom was an intruder who took her son away and had no place in this family. I never liked my grandma, and she never liked me or my brothers. She was very happy and called it God's punishment when Mom gave birth to a beautiful baby girl who only lived for twenty-four hours. She would be my oldest sister; her name was Erika. Mom was heartbroken, and it took three years before she had another child. My brother Jorg was born, and a year later I came.

My dad loved my mom and told his mother to stay out of his marriage. His mom was furious and tried every trick to interfere. I can't remember how many times she tried to tell me how bad my mom was. One year we went to see her on Christmas, and we had to wait at the railroad station to be picked up. We had a suitcase full of presents, and I began to open one package after another. My brother was not interested in opening the suitcase, but nothing could stop me.

When grandma came, she was very angry, and she shouted at me and told me that we would get nothing for Christmas. She said it was God's punishment because we were bad just like our mother. Dad had sent all our presents to his mother because he knew that I would open the suitcase, but Grandma gave all the things to my cousin; she was her favored granddaughter, and her mom was Grandmother's youngest daughter. Well, this was typical for her.

When she came to visit us, she gave my brothers and me a handful of candies and went with us to the store to buy all kinds of expensive outfits, toys, and books for her special granddaughter. It was not very nice, and I never forgot how much I was hurting. This is one of the main reasons I never treat my grandchildren differently; I love each one the same way, and they know it.

I can only remember my grandmother when I was a child. When I got older, I refused to visit her, and she didn't want to see my mom. My grandfather had nothing to say; he had to do what his wife said, and so we lost all contact because my dad stood behind his family.

I will now stop this chapter about my grandmother and will tell you more about my family. But first, I'd like to mark some important dates I need to remember in my story.

It was the beginning of World War II. The terrible Kristal night where thousands of Jews were tortured and brutally killed was November 9, 1938. It was the beginning of the Holocaust. This should and will never be forgotten. It should be a reminder for the whole world what happens when people hate. Germany became an enemy to the world.

The first bombing of Bochum, the city where I was born, and other cities began on May 13, 1943, and lasted until June 4, 1943. The final and last bombing, which I still remember, was 1944. It was when Bochum, Essen, Dortmund, and Gelsenkirchen were totally destroyed. More than five thousand people lost their lives. Every city was burning. World War II started September 1, 1939, and the war was over May 7, 1945. Almost all the big cities were up to eighty percent gone, and only the small villages were untouched by the bombing and miraculously saved. Today, all the villages are the main attraction for any visitor, because of the old beauty and ancient, historic buildings and churches. Besides, the azure-blue sea surrounded by high mountains with everlasting snow and ice will call any visitor to come back again.

2

World War II: Loss and a New Home

In 1939, when I was born, Germany was not as beautiful as it had been. These were bad times, and the country was ready for World War II—a war that would affect the whole world, a war that killed millions of innocent people both young and old, a war that left behind nothing but chaos, pain, tears, and bitterness.

My parents weren't rich; my dad worked for the railroad and also was a sports teacher, and when my brother was born he was hoping to pass sports on to him. But Jorg was afraid of getting hurt and screamed from the top of his lungs when Dad tried to lift him up on his shoulder or lift him up in the air.

When I came along, my brother was thirteen months old, and soon my dad started to hold me up high and was surprised that I didn't scream and cry. I couldn't get enough, and my dad was proud of me. I missed him very much when he had to leave to fight for the war of Adolf Hitler. I can't remember when all the big cities were burned down, but I can remember when every night and day the sirens would call us to the bunker and bomb shelter. I still remember when Opa and Mom took us to the shelter night after night, and we had to sit on a bench and wait to get back to our home. I will never ever forget when my home and city were destroyed and we lost everything.

So I think I will skip the first four years of my life and start my story when I was about five years old. Opa was not able to live with us, and since we had lost everything, we needed a new place to stay and be safe.

Mom decided to leave the city and move to the country. It was a different place, and we had to wait for people to be willing to open their homes and give shelter to needy families. We were waiting in the courthouse in a town called Luedenscheid, and it took a long time. Mom was tired and thought she had to wait another day, but when she was ready to leave she couldn't find me and Jorg. She was afraid that we were lost and began to look for us. She turned around and an older man stopped her and ask her why she was so upset. Mother told him that she was looking for her two children.

The man smiled and said, "The little girl is outside, and she and her brother are with Polly, my horse. I love children and I think you will love my wife and our home. You need a good meal and a good night's rest. If you decide not to stay, it is okay. Come with me, and we will take care of the paperwork tomorrow."

I know Mom was relieved and knew right away that God was taking care of us. This man was kind and smiled; he was very understanding and would help her and the children. Also, Mother had special privileges because she had two little children and her husband was fighting on the front lines. But she had already made her decision and agreed to take the helping hand from this nice man. He helped her into the carriage, and after he made sure that we were all happy, he whistled and the horse began to pull the carriage. We had a great time, and Mom began to relax and fell asleep.

I don't know how long the ride was but I liked to listen to the horse Polly. She was old but very gentle and always ready when she was needed. We stopped in front of a very nice farm house. Mom woke up, and the man helped her again. He said, "I'd like to welcome you all to our home. You can call me Paul Wertman or Pa—that is shorter." He opened a heavy oak door and shouted, "Ma, come and greet our new guests! I don't know their names, but they need a good meal and a warm bed. The young lady fell asleep, but her little children are very nice. The little girl talked to me all the time. The little boy is a bit shy, but I think he is also very hungry."

Ma Wertman was a wonderful person—jolly, hearty, and full of humor. Pa Wertman was about fifty, fat and round like a ball, but extremely nice and kind. He had a warm smile and always a treat for

Jorg and me. He called us "his little children." Ma was very concerned about us, and every morning she would bring us a big basket filled with fresh, juicy fruit, crisp lettuce, or deep, red tomato, she had just picked early in the morning in her huge garden.

Ma Wertman loved to surprise Mother and help to heal the wounds of this bloody war. They really tried to bring sunshine in our life. Almost every morning Pa Wertman took us children out in the woods where we listened to the birds and picked berries and wild flowers until it started to get cold and the first snow came. But we were safe and didn't pay very much attention to the war.

We were having a wonderful time with the Wertman's, but outside, only about fifty miles away, people were losing their loved ones, their lives, and their homes. The war wasn't over, and people were in constant fear of the next attack. It was December 23, 1944. It was almost Christmas, and my dad was still not home; I missed him very much. Mother sat in the kitchen and read a story to us.

All of a sudden we were interrupted by a loud banging on the door. I grabbed Mom's apron and Jorg hid under the table. Mother went to open the door. The noise had stopped, and Mother couldn't believe her eyes. Ma and Pa Wertman had decorated a little tree with delicious candies, home-baked cookies, handmade, tiny little candles, and gorgeous angels and stars made out of thin paper. Both sang, "Silent Night, Holy Night." It was a wonderful surprise, and Mother was crying. Ma and Pa had a great voice, and I never forgot that day. I never forget the words Pa said to mother: "You and the children are invited to celebrate Christmas with us tomorrow. No one who lives under our roof is allowed to be unhappy on Christmas and the Holy Night. This is a tradition in our family."

Pa Wertman sat the tree very carefully on the table; he put his arm around me and Jorg and said, "You know that God loves all the children, and we celebrate Jesus' birthday tomorrow."

On December 24, 1944, Mother dressed Jorg and me in clean outfits; we only had one outfit, so Mother had to put us to bed when she needed to wash our clothes. Jorg and I had to spend almost the whole day in bed.

Now we were dressed and ready. Mom gave us instruction on how to behave: "Don't go on anything, try to be good, ask before you touch items, and say please and thank you."

Clang, clang, rang the bell through the hall. This was the sign for us to come down. Mom was a little nervous, and she tried to hold us back. I can't forget the moment we came into the good room. A huge eight-foot, perfect tree was decorated with silver stars and straw stars, with bells and glitter and many handmade white candles. The Christmas tree was placed in the corner of the room across from the fire place. Under the tree was a stable with a little light. It was filled with figures carved out of wood and hand painted in all different colors. Mary and Joseph and the little baby Jesus and many sheep, shepherds, cows, angels, and the three kings were carefully placed under the tree and in the stable. Mary had an azure blue cape over her shoulder and Joseph was holding a tiny lamp, which gave the light in the stable.

On a fresh bundle of straw and hay in a small manger was a sweet little baby with curly hair wrapped in swaddling clothes. He had a beautiful face and rosy cheeks and smiled at us. It was just too much. Jorg and I could not stop; we kneeled down and stared at all the figures. We forgot all our promises to be good and to ask before we touched anything—we just had to play with all the figures. We took the shepherds and the sheep and placed them in the stable. We set the angels on the roof made out of straw and moved the three kings closer to the stable. Mom was embarrassed but Pa laughed and told her not to worry and to enjoy it all.

"It's Christmas and Christmas is for children. You see, your boy and your little girl are very happy, and they enjoy playing with all the figures. This Nativity set is very old and many children played with it. Look at your little girl; she loves Jesus."

I took Jesus out and gave him a kiss, and then I held the beautiful little figure in the palm of my hand, and whispered, "Please, Jesus, bring Daddy home!"

Very carefully I placed him back and gave Ma and Pa Wertman a big hug and said thank you to both for letting us play with Jesus.

After the excitement was settled, Ma and Pa brought a big basket and handed us many packages wrapped in white paper with hand-painted stars and our names. We began to open one package after the next, and each one was a surprise. There were new mittens, a beautiful scarf for me and a warm stocking cap for Jorg, a new handmade dress and slippers for me, and shoes, stockings and underwear for both of us. Jorg also got a wooden truck with animals and tiny, colorful farm figures. Ma Wertman handed me a porcelain doll dressed like little red riding hood. She said, "Alusru, I want you to have this doll. You need to be very careful, but you can play with her and love her. I played with her when I was a little girl just like you."

I have to say Ma Wertman had a golden heart, and I loved her very much.

My mom also received many gifts—some clothes, silverware, dishes and all kinds of homemade jam and other food items. My mother was in tears and gave everyone a hug. She took her necklace she was wearing and gave it to Ma Wertman. She said, "I want you to have this. I don't have anything else but this, and you are so wonderful to us. You took us into your home and treated us like family. You helped the children to forget the bloody war and showered us all with wonderful gifts."

Mother put the necklace into Ma Wertman's hand and gave her a big hug. Ma Wertman hesitated to accept the gift and said, "Are you sure you like to give this beautiful heart necklace to me? I think you should keep it because I think this is from your husband."

But mother insisted and told her that it was from her Papa, and he would be very proud to see it on Ma Wertman's neck. "I hope one day you will be meeting my Papa," she said.

It was an unforgettable Christmas Day, and our hearts were filled with happiness. Meanwhile, the world was still on fire and no word from Daddy. After the distribution of the presents and the hugs and tears, we all gathered around the fire place. Ma served a delicious dinner—stuffed goose with purple plums, apples, and dumplings, and red cabbage. She also had a variety of fresh fruit and raw veggies. The grown-ups had coffee, and Jorg and I had fresh goat milk. For dessert we had a butter cream torte.

We gave thanks to the Lord, and Ma and Pa invited us to accompany them to the midnight service at the little Hill Church. Mother bundled Jorg and me in new clothes, and Pa Wertman went to get the sleigh ready. Jorg and I sat in front with Pa and Ma sat in the back with Mother. Pa whistled and Polly, the white horse, started to pull the sleigh. Pa had decorated her with little silver bells around her neck. I still remember how much I enjoyed to listen to the soft sound of the ringing bells and the clang, clang of her hooves. In the last few hours, the sky had opened and the earth was covered with a soft, fluffy, white blanket. But now only a few flakes were dancing from the sky. Indeed it was a special White Christmas!

Soon Polly stopped at the church. Pa helped us out of the sleigh, and we all entered the foyer of the church. Candlelight, the smell of fresh evergreen, and the soft sound of organ music welcomed us. Pastor Konig brought the holy message to the congregation. He urged the people to pray for an end to the war and to bring peace to the whole world.

A small group of children sang a few Christmas songs and lit some candles. Then the pastor asked everyone to turn to the person next to them and give them a hug and wish them the best. He lifted his hands to ask God to bless everyone.

Jorg and I were fascinated and forgot to follow Mother and the Wertmans. Pastor Konig came and put his hand on my shoulder. He asked us what we wished to tell God we wanted for Christmas. I looked at the pastor and told him without hesitation I wished my daddy would come home. I missed him very much. My brother also wished the same; he is very shy, but he told me that he wanted Daddy to come home.

Jorg looked at the pastor and nodded his head. He took my hand and Pastor Konig walked with us to the altar. I think he had tears in his eyes when he said, "Alusru and Jorg, let us pray and ask Jesus to bring your daddy home."

I looked at the cross over the altar and folded my hands. I went down on my knees and pulled my brother down. I closed my eyes and said, "Dear Jesus, I love You. Can You please tell my daddy to come home? I will give You some cookies. I have five cookies and I will give You three and I will also give You two from Jorg if he didn't eat them. Please, Jesus, can You bring Daddy home? I promise to try to be good. I love You, Jesus, and Pa and Ma Wertman, Mother and Opa, and the pastor, Amen!"

Pastor Konig gave us a hug and told us to pray every day. I nudged Jorg and said, "You have to help me. Maybe God will listen to you."

Jorg tried to pray, "P-p-please, God, bring Daddy home. Amen!"

Pastor Konig smiled and said, "God can do anything, and He can bring your daddy home to you and your mom. Let's go outside; I think your mom is looking for you."

My heart was filled with joy. Could it be possible that God was able to bring Daddy home? Pa Wertman came back at this time, and he was glad when he discovered us in the church. I think he was a little worried about us that we were lost. The two men shook hands and Pastor Konig wished us all a very peaceful and happy Christmas. Most of the people were already gone. Polly waited patiently, and Ma and Mother were sitting in the sleigh. We climbed up and Pa put a blanket around us. It was cold. Pa gave Polly the order to move. The snow made a crunchy noise and Polly had first a difficult time to pull the sleigh. Her bells rang through the white winter wonderland. The temperature had dropped, and some of the snow had turned to ice. Nobody said a word.

Jorg and I felt very tired, but we were also so excited. Was it really true? Could God bring Daddy home? Does God answer prayers? Yes, we will pray every day and maybe God will answer if I give Him all of my and Jorg's cookies. I decided to talk to my brother and to tell him that he can't eat his cookies. We didn't know at this time at this very moment that God was already in charge and Daddy was on his way home. It was another miracle that only God could give, because He heard a child's prayer. Mother helped me to undress my new doll and Jorg played with his new truck.

3

Christmas 1944: A Stranger, a Hero, and the Lord

It was December 26, 1944, second Christmas Day (in Germany we celebrate Christmas two days). Jorg tried to load up his farm animals when Pa Wertman called us down for a fresh glass of goat milk and chocolate cookies. We ran downstairs, and of course Ma also gave us some candies. I took my cookies and put them in my apron and tried to take Jorg's, too, but he refused and held on to each one. Ma was surprised and asked astonished, "What in the world is wrong with you Alusru? Don't you like to eat my cookies? And why did you try to take the cookies from your brother?"

I tried to find a good answer, and I looked at Ma, embarrassed. I said, "Oh, I like your cookies and I thank you very much, but I can't eat them because the cookies belong to Jesus. I promised Jesus all of my and Jorg's cookies if he brings Daddy home. You see, I really like to eat the cookies but I made a deal with Jesus, and I have to keep my promise."

"Well, sweetheart, I think I have to give you two extra cookies and I know Jesus wants you to eat them; he wants to share them with you."

Ma took a large piece of fire wood and tried to put it into the black, smoky fireplace. It was very difficult to do since there was almost no space for another piece of wood. I think she was crying and didn't want us to see her tears.

Pa Wertman called and told us to dress warm; he wanted to take us out for a short walk. Mother brought our new coats, mittens, scarves, and hats. We went outside and tried to build a snowman. I tried to talk Jorg into giving me his cookies, but my brother didn't agree with me and ate them all. He shook his head when I tried to explain to him if we have lots of cookies to give to Jesus, God would answer our prayer faster. It was very cold. The crystals of the snow blinded us for a moment. We walked down the hill holding on to Pa's hand. New snow had fallen, and it was not very cold. It was about three in the afternoon.

All we saw was a little dog chasing after a brownish cat, and a man some distance from us. Pa looked and said, "I wonder who that man is; I don't think I have seen him before. It must be a stranger. Well, we will see. I know almost everyone in this area. He is walking in our direction. Let's see who he is. Maybe he is lost and looking for someone."

Pa put his hand over his eyes to get a better look at the man, but he still couldn't identify the stranger. "No, I don't know that person," he said.

Jorg and I didn't look at the man, and we paid no attention to him. We tried to stop the big dog from chasing that little cat, and we threw a snowball at the dog. It stopped him catching that frightened cat, and she went up the tree. I think she was happy, and the dog had no chance to catch her.

The stranger came closer and looked at us. He also put his hand over his eyes to try to see better. He stopped and then he called out to us: "Alusru, Jorg!" Again, "Alusru, Jorg, is it really you?"

He called again our names and tried to walk faster. I didn't know who the man was and Jorg didn't know him either. He shook his head. The man came closer and called our names again. Pa Wertman called out to him and tried to find out who he was. The man was only a few steps away from us and Pa saw that he was exhausted. I didn't know him, and I was afraid. He had a beard and long black hair and his clothes were dirty. He looked kind of scary.

Who was this man? He was wearing a uniform and he knew our names. Pa Wertman took the stranger by his arm and said, "Whoever you are, you need some help, a good night's sleep, and a hearty meal. The kids don't know you, and you thought maybe you know them. I will take you to our home and help you. We have enough room and enough to eat."

The man was unable to resist and took Pa's hand. I was still afraid and held on to Jorg and Pa. We didn't said anything, and I could feel the pounding of my heart when we entered the hall. Pa called out for Ma. She came into the hall and looked at the strange man. Pa told her that the man was exhausted and needed a good warm bed and a meal.

"I think we still have some stuffed goose left, and he can rest for a while. The room upstairs can be heated, and I will get you some bricks and heat them in the oven. By the way the man knew the children's name. He called Alusru and Jorg, but the kids have no idea who he is. I think he is a soldier and he needs some help. It is still Christmas, and maybe we can help him to get back on his feet. We have enough food and also enough room."

The man looked at us, and again he said our names. Ma Wertman agreed with her husband and said, "Oh my goodness, he must have walked a long way without food. He looks very tired. Perhaps he is a friend of the family. Alusru, call your mom. Maybe she can help us. Maybe she knows who the stranger is; go and tell her to come down."

Jorg and I went to get Mother. We went upstairs, and I shouted, "Mama, Mama, we have company, and Ma Wertman wants you to meet the man. He has a beard, long black hair, and a dirty uniform, but we don't know who he is. He knew Jorg and me."

Mother said, "I don't know anybody here, and Opa doesn't have black hair and a beard. Well, I'll see."

Mother looked in the mirror, ran a comb through her beautiful blond hair, straightened out her apron, and came down the stairs. As she entered the hall, her steps were hesitant. She looked at the stranger, and I will never forget the moment when she saw his face. She tried to lean against the big oak door. Her face turned white and her lips lost all their red color. Then, with a scream, Mother fell on the floor.

The strange man rushed over to Mother. He lifted her head up and kissed her over and over again. With every kiss he repeated Mother's name: "Oh, Anna Margret, my dear Anna Margret, everything is good now. I found you and the children. We will make it. The war is soon over. Oh, I love you so much, and I missed you all."

Mother opened her eyes, and suddenly she kissed the stranger right on his beard and laughed and cried. She put her arms around him and under tears and laughter she called him by his name: "Martin, oh Martin, I can't believe it is you. I missed you every day, and I love you so much."

I think Mother forgot all about us, and finally Ma and Pa Wertman came to Mother and helped her up. Pa also gave the stranger a big hug and Ma began to cry. Jorg and I looked at the adults. We still didn't know who this stranger was and why everybody laugh and cried.

Who was that man? Mother looked at Jorg and me, and our faces with the question mark; Jorg and I were very much puzzled. Why did Mama fall on the floor, and why is everyone crying?

Mother gave us a hug and took us to the stranger. She laughed when we hesitated to look at him, and then she said, "Jorg and Alusru, this is your daddy. Your daddy came home. I can't believe it, but it is true. Your daddy is home. Come and give your daddy a big hug and kiss."

I wasn't sure, and when I looked at the man my mom called my daddy, I said only, "Jesus answered our prayer, and the pastor was right. He told us to ask Jesus, and I asked Him and promised to give all my cookies to Him. You see, Jorg, why I needed your cookies? If you hadn't given me some of your cookies Daddy would not have come home until tomorrow. Ma I have to give all of my cookies to Jesus. I made a promise and I have to keep my promise, but where can I find Jesus?"

I looked at Pa and Ma Wertman and began to cry. "Pa, where can I find Jesus? Can we go to the church and ask the pastor? He must know where Jesus is. Please, Pa. Can Polly bring me to the church?"

Pa smiled, took me on his lap and said, "Of course we must go to the church, and I think Jesus will answer you. But first we will all pray and give thanks to God. Also, your daddy needs a good meal and you need to give him a big hug and kiss."

Tears ran down his face when Pa took me over to my daddy. I thought, *everyone is crying*, and I started to cry when Daddy held me in his arms and whispered my name over and over. No doubt this was Daddy, even though he had a beard. I said, "Thank you, Jesus. Thank you, God. I love you, Jesus, and I will give you all of my cookies. I don't know where I can find you, but I think you can send angels to the church. I will put all my cookies under the tree. Sorry, Jesus, but Jorg ate most of his cookies. I think you understand, and I know he loves you."

It was very quiet, and I could see that Daddy was crying. Jorg looked at me and smiled.

Ring, ring, ring, rang the big bell through the hall. "Who could that be?" Pa said, and went to open the door.

I was still very excited, but I followed Pa while Ma took my daddy to the big table with all kinds of food. She also brought some warm shirts, pants, socks, and slippers she had found in the attic and told Daddy to try them on later.

When Pa opened the door, I saw two little children—a boy and a girl. The girl was the oldest child—about seven or eight—and she carried a small basket. She looked at me and tried to smile. She said, "Please, Mr. Wertman, forgive us that we bother you on Christmas, but our mom is sick and Mama said to ask you for some bread. You see, we are hungry, and when Mama feels better, she will do some work for you."

I looked at the girl and felt sorry for her when I saw her tears. The little girl tried to stop crying, and her big eyes looked at Pa when she whispered, "It is okay if you don't have enough for all of us, but it is Christmas and I will give Mama all the food because she needs to get better."

The girl tried to be strong and to wipe the tears away. Her hands were dirty and her face had dirt all over. The little boy took her hand, and Pa gave both kids a big hug and called Ma, telling her that Susan and Bert, Laura's two children, came to let her know that their mom was sick and that both kids were very hungry. Ma came and told the kids that she didn't know their mom was sick, and of course she would give them food. Also, she and Pa would come and see her soon. She took the basket and filled it with bread, fresh rolls, cookies, and fruit. Pa said, "I will bring you more food tomorrow, and tell your mom we will all pray for her to get well."

All of a sudden I had a warm feeling, and my heart started to pound in my chest. I looked at Susan, smiled and said, "I have some cookies, and I will give all to you. You see, our daddy came home and we had prayed to God and Jesus to bring Daddy home. I told Jesus that I would give Him all of my cookies if Daddy came home. Jesus answered my prayers and Jorg's. Daddy came home today. I promised all my cookies to Jesus, but I really don't know where I can find Him. Last time I saw Him in the manger, I thought if I put the cookies in the straw an angel would come and bring them to Jesus, but I think He wouldn't mind if I give all of my cookies to your mom and to you and your brother."

I took a paper and put the cookies on it. Some were still crunchy, but most were soft and partially broken. My brother also had two cookies left, and he gave each cookie to Bert and smiled at me. A happy smile appeared on both kids' faces when we put all the goodies in their basket. Susan gave me a hug, and all she could say was thank you. She and her brother went to the door, and Susan turned around, looked at me and whispered, "Alusru, I'll tell Jesus that you gave His cookies to my mom, Bert, and me."

Both kids said thank you again. Bert told his sister that this was the best Christmas and that they both have to ask Jesus to make their mom better. "Mom will be so happy, and she will be okay soon. The kids left, and we could hear both singing, "Merry Christmas to all."

Ma and Pa Wertman decided to give Mom and Dad some time for themselves. They told us to come into the kitchen. We looked at Daddy. We agreed to let Mother be with Daddy and were ready to leave, but Dad told us to stay because he had something to tell—something so wonderful that he needed to share it with us right away. He called it a wonderful, great miracle—a miracle that can only come from God. "Please, I would like you to stay and listen to how God can work miracles."

I looked at my dad and said, "God did another miracle? Whatever it is, Daddy, you came home, and I think that was a great miracle. Did you tell God you would give Him some cookies if he helped you to get home?"

Everyone laughed and Daddy gave me a kiss. He said, "No, sweetie, I didn't have cookies; all I could do was pray and talk to God. He will always listen, and He will answer in His way and time. So when you pray to God, listen, and I think He will smile when you try to bargain with Him. Now, let me tell you all what happened to me when I was on my way home. I think God listened to my little girl and boy when they prayed, and God was watching over me when my life was in danger. He surrounded our troops with His angels.

"One day we were on the east side of Germany in a little village, and all the people gathered together in a very old, small church. The people insisted that we all stay in the church. The Russian army was not far away, and we could hear the shouting and yelling. We thought it was very foolish to seek shelter at a church. It was very cold and heavy snow came down too late to look for another shelter. I thought we would all get killed. The pastor told us to talk to God and ask Him for protection. All the people were asking God over and over again, *Eine Mauer um uns baue* (Please, God, build a wall so the enemy cannot find us).

"Most of the soldiers didn't believe in God and also didn't know what to say. They laughed at the ones who prayed. Some wanted to leave but were unable to do so. After two days, and without any attack from the enemy, almost everyone was praying, and after three days we decided to leave the church. We couldn't hear any noise and everyone thought the Russian troops went in another direction.

"The pastor tried to open the door and all we could see was a huge wall surrounding the small village. It was a snow wall and a heavy snow blanket had covered every house and all the buildings. Everyone started to praise and worship God because God had answered their prayers. We went all on our knees and the soldiers who had laughed at God and the people who weren't praying were sobbing and crying asking God for forgiveness.

"A few days later, we found many bodies, guns, and ammunition. God stopped the army in His way. The village was never touched, and the people buried all the dead Russian soldiers. When we found out about the bad things Adolf Hitler was doing to our country, and to so many innocent people, we all decided to leave the army and to hide until the war was over. In other words, we deserted from the troops and became fugitives. Each one of us had to find his own way and protection.

"Some soldiers decided to stay in the village and others went to find a way to their home town. We all gathered together in the church, and the people brought us food and blankets to take along on our long journey. The pastor told us to trust God and to ask Him when we are feeling danger and when we are tired and hungry. God will answer because He is able to open doors we can't see, and He can feed us in our sleep. All we have to do is trust Him and believe. Without God, I would not be here today.

"I can't tell you how often I prayed and how often I wanted to give up, but God heard my prayer every time, and when I was exhausted He brought me to a safe place and put me to sleep. When I was hungry, He gave me food to eat; sometimes it was berries I found in the woods, other times I stopped to catch fish in a nearby river, or I found a helping hand in another town. I knew I could always look to Him.

"When I was walking in the wrong direction, God pulled me away from the danger, and I thanked Him every time. I also asked God to protect you all and to give you the help to be safe. God told me to 'be still; to trust Him and know that He is God!' And I know that God took care of you and brought you to this place.

"When I look at this wonderful home and see the faces of all you, I have to thank the Lord that He brought you to this lovely home because I feel that Ma and Pa Wertman are wonderful people who love the Lord. I trust the Lord and I will always trust Him. Today I can tell you God loves you no matter what. The miracle at the village was great, but the second miracle was wonderful, and I call it awesome because I could see His glory when I was in a great danger, almost killed by guns pointed at me not far from here because I was a fugitive without any identification.

"A troop of American Soldiers stopped me. They asked me for my papers, but I had no papers, and I knew without any identification being stopped by a military troop was bad. I could be shot or become a prisoner. I trusted God again and prayed in my heart. The commander spoke very good German, and he was not very old. He said, 'Mister, are you a soldier? I need to see your pass papers.'

"My first thought was to get ready to run, but he pulled his gun and shouted, 'You know that I can give the order to shoot you.'

"I told him, 'I agree, and before you kill me, please let me look at the picture of my children.'

"I tried to pull the letter out but the officer didn't trust me and shouted, 'Keep your hands up; I will reach in your pocket, and you can look at the picture, but this will be all I let you do.'

"He reached into my coat pocket and pulled out a letter. It fell on the ground and he picked it up. He said something I couldn't understand because I prayed to God to help me. When the commander questioned me again I felt no fear. I looked at him and was surprised that he wanted to know why I had an Air Mail letter from the United States in my pocket. I told him that this was a letter from Detroit,

Michigan, from my brother George. The officer turned the letter and saw my brother's address.

"The next thing was when I felt God's hand. The commander pulled out the picture from both of you and Mom, and also a picture of my brother. He said with tears in his eyes, 'I can't believe it, I can't believe that George is your brother. George and I have been roommates for a long time, he told me that he had family in Germany and this is our address. I will do anything I can to get you back to your wife and children because your brother is my best friend; we have known each other for a very long time. I know you are not an enemy to our country, so I will help you.'

"He gave a few orders to his soldiers and called for his Jeep. He told me to sit back and not to worry. The troop took off. We had no problems, and at the camp, he gave me an old uniform and then he drove me to the safe zone. When he left, he said, 'The war will soon be over, and when I have a chance, I will visit you. Take care, and tell everyone Black Joe from Michigan wishes all a Merry Christmas and God's blessing.'

"He gave me a hug, turned his Jeep around, and disappeared. I went on my knees and cried. I was free and only a few miles away from all of you, and I thanked God and asked Him for His guidance. I felt that God was right on my side, and when I turned the wrong way, I was unable to walk until I changed my direction. When I left the deep woods, I heard laughter and saw children playing in the snow. I was exhausted and didn't know that it was my two sweet little children, but God told me to call your names and I called you: 'Alusru, Jorg,' again and again. You know the rest."

It was very still. Our dad had been talking the whole time, and no one said a word. He was holding Jorg and me in his arms, and I didn't care that he had a beard and his hair was long. He was my daddy, and I loved him very much. I put my arms around his neck and kissed him. I told him that I really missed him and that I always love him.

Daddy was crying. The chimes of the old grandfather clock rang out, and we were all brought back to reality. Pa Wertman was the first one who broke the silence. He got up and said, "I'll get the sleigh ready, and you all get ready; we have to go to church. This is a great miracle, and God is with us. We have to thank Him and the church is God's house."

We all agreed, and in no time everyone was sitting in the sleigh, covered with a warm blanket. The snow was very deep and it was bitterly cold. Polly had a difficult time pulling the happy load, and she stopped often. After a while, we could see the little church on the hill. The cross on the steeple was golden and looked like it was surrounded by beautiful light.

Pa stopped the sleigh in front of the church close to pastor Konig's house. We all entered the house of God and walked to the altar. Pastor Konig and his wife Edith came; they were surprised to see us. Jorg and I kneeled down by the manger. Mary, Joseph, the three kings, the shepherds, the sheep, and all the angels were there. I looked at the little baby Jesus, touched His cheek, and began to cry. I said, "I am so sorry, little baby Jesus. I promised You all my cookies, but I don't have any cookies to give to You because I gave them all to Susan, Bert, and their mom. I didn't know where I could find You. I am so sorry, Jesus, that I didn't keep my promise, but they were so hungry."

I couldn't stop my tears, and it felt good when the pastor's wife put her hand on my shoulder and told me that I did the right thing. Then she pointed to the baby in the manger and said, "Look Alusru, Jesus is happy. He is smiling at you. Jesus will understand. All He wants is for you to love Him, thank Him, and trust Him. Remember He will always love you. God has a wonderful way to bring His sheep home.

"God did not want this war. God loves His children, and sometimes a wonder or miracle appears to assure us how much God loves this world, because God created everything. After all, *God is love!* And God's love created you and me and all the beautiful things on Earth. I can tell you, Alusru, that God is very happy that you gave your cookies to Susan, her brother, and her mother. You are a good little girl, and you did the right thing."

I still remember the manger and the sweet little baby smiling at me. Oh yes, I did the right thing, and I know Jesus would have done the same. To this day, I always feel happy when I surprise people and see them smile.

My brother gave me a hug and smiled. I don't know how long we all gave praise and thanks to the Lord, but my dad shared God's guidance and miracles with the pastor and his wife. Pastor Koenig said that God was watching over my dad, and my dad had asked God for help and trusted Him in every way. Only God was able to protect him and bring him home to his family.

But also the prayer from two little children were answered the same time. I think without God's help my daddy would never come home. When we left, it was very cold and Jorg and I sat in the back of the sleigh cuddled up in warm blankets and holding onto each other. The sky was covered with many stars, and no one said a word. Daddy was home and we didn't have to be worried anymore. I had the feeling that this was all a dream and a fairy tale. Maybe the war was over and every dad would be home soon.

But the reality was the war was still not over, and Dad needed to be very careful because he was still a fugitive. Pa Wertman took care of everything. Dad made furniture and helped to repair things. I have to say my dad was very handy. He could make very nice tables, cabinets, and chairs, and fixed almost anything that was broken. We had a great time.

But the war was not over, and it took more than five months for it to come to an end. People from all over came to celebrate May 5, 1945, the end of the bloody war.

Ma and Pa Wertman and Mother went to the city hall, and Dad stayed at the farm with us because Mother didn't want us to go along, and Pa thought it was a good decision. The war was finally over, and every street was decorated to welcome the American troops. Most people went to the guest house "Rose" to celebrate the end of the war.

Jorg and I were not very happy that we had to stay home. We would have rather gone with all the others, but Pa Wertman told us that we were too young and it was better for us to stay home. This was final, and there was no more discussion. Dad was more than happy to stay with us. He gave us some paper for drawing and coloring, and soon we forgot all about the celebration—although at times we could hear the street music, laughing, and singing.

All of the sudden, the music stopped and it was very, very still. Jorg and I stopped coloring, and Dad went to the window. "Maybe someone is giving a speech to the crowd," Dad said. "Come, kids, finish your picture."

But this was a wrong guess. A few minutes later, we heard two shots and ringing through the air, and then many more following. It sound like a detonation. Not very far away, we heard someone yell, "What on Earth was that?"

Then there was screaming and yelling with many more shots, then silence. It seemed to me to echo, even when the shots stopped.

Dad opened the window. "Maybe the war was still not over," Dad said. Who fired the shots? No one is permitted to have any weapon and these were shots fired with a machine gun. We were very much puzzled, but not for long. Dad looked out the window.

"Daddy, can you see what is wrong? Please, please say something that has happened. Why did the music stop? Are the people not happy anymore?" I asked.

Dad didn't answer, and somehow I felt sad and was afraid. I started to cry and Jorg cried also. Daddy closed the window, put his arms around us, and said, "We will soon find out what happened because I saw mother and the Wertman's coming back. Something is not right, but you both don't have to be afraid. Soon we will all have the answers, so let's wait for Mother and Ma and Pa Wertman."

We sat down and looked at Daddy. Was Daddy also afraid? Our thoughts were far away when Ma and Pa and Mother came back.

"What has happened? Why did everyone rush home? Did someone get hurt? Is the war over?"

We looked at Mother. She had tears in her eyes and looked very sad. Pa Wertman said, "I am so glad that the kids stayed home because it was very bad."

He told Daddy the details of what happened but never really let us know. Many years later, I found out everything, and I am glad that he kept it away from us. Something very sad happened, and today I still can't believe it because this was almost a hate act or bitter racism. It was still unbelievable and caused an entire town to mourn. Besides, many people did not believe that America tried to help Germany. The people were afraid to let others know they had relatives living in the United States of America.

The war was over, but a young boy who loved the American soldiers was killed in cold blood by a black American Sergeant. As soon as everyone entered the Guest House "Rose," the owner Jack Halverson shouted, "The American troops are coming; let's all go outside and greet them."

Everyone followed Jack. His son Timmy and few of Timmy's friends had rolled a small tree stump across Main Street, and they had painted in big letters the words: WELCOME AMERICA! WELCOME TO FREEDOM! The American troops were coming. Everyone was waiting and waved little American flags made out of paper. We all tried to sing: America, America.

The first tanker came and then four, five, six Jeeps, behind another tanker, and a column of big trucks, loaded with soldiers. There was the tree! The first tanker did not stop, but six Jeeps now pulled over to the side. A very heavy-set black officer climbed out of the first Jeep. He looked at the crowd and shouted, "Who put the tree on the street?"

He had his hand on his weapon. Timmy stepped forward and with a proud voice he said, "I did it, and we like to welcome America and you and all of the soldiers."

Timmy's English wasn't very good and many soldiers laughed. The officer pulled his pistol. He was very angry, and before anyone was really able to understand the situation, he aimed his weapon at Timmy and fired many shots. Timmy lay in his own blood on the street, clutching the American flag in his hand.

The white letters he had painted were not white anymore. Timmy's blood changed the color to red. Some tried to attack the black officer, but he took a machine gun and fired several shots shouting, "I hope you all get the message, and this will teach you all a lesson. No one can stop the American troops!"

Again he fired several shots, climbed back in his Jeep, gave a few commands to the troop, and every soldier lifted their gun up, pointing at the people. Everyone was afraid, and no one tried to welcome the Americans anymore.

Jack and Rita Halverson and a few others took the body of Timmy and brought him in the Guest House. All the people were in shock and Rita broke down. She was holding her only child in her arms. She cried and people were asking questions: What will be the future for Germany? Was this Peace? Who can answer all the questions?

Timmy was dead, killed for no reason. He loved America!

Two days later, he was laid to rest, and with him, so many people's love for America. But his parents fulfilled the last wish he had shared with his friends: "If I die in an accident, I would like the American flag on my grave."

When I visited Timmy's grave I saw a big flag pole with the American and German flag, and on a stone plate were the words *Hate will kill! Love has no enemy!* Yes, Timmy died and he was only seventeen. He died because in his heart was only love—love for a country he had never seen, love for soldiers who were ordered to throw bombs on Germany.

I know that he was a hero. His friends and family told everyone that Timmy always helped other kids to be a friend. I don't know if the black officer was ever punished for what he did, but I think from what I have learned about Timmy, he would ask everyone to forgive him, because he loved everyone and was a follower of Jesus Christ! Ask yourself, *What would Jesus do?* He loves us all!

4

A New Town, a New Home, and a Goodbye

The war was over, and we had to say goodbye to Pa and Ma Wertman because Daddy found a new place. We had to move to Altena in Westphalia because it was close to the railroad station, and he had received a job offer to work for the railroad. It was a very big change for Jorg and me, and I was not very happy because I missed Ma and Pa Wertman very much. Jorg didn't care, and he was not crying when we left. I was very upset with my brother because he was very anxious to move. I missed Polly the old horse, my friends, the farm house, the walk in the woods, the warm goat milk, and the delicious cookies and hugs and kisses from Ma and Pa. In other words, I missed everything and was not very nice to my parents. Many times I said things just to let my anger and frustration out and did not realize how much I hurt my parents with my words. But I think one day I went too far when I said to my dad, "This is all your fault; we would have never moved here if you hadn't come home."

My mother was very angry with me. She told me, "I will not let you talk like that; you know it was a miracle that your daddy came home. Many children have to grow up without a daddy because their father never came home from the war. You need to apologize to your daddy and ask Jesus to forgive you and help you control your anger."

I remember my dad gave me a big hug and said, "I know, Alusru. You didn't want to say that and you really didn't mean everything you said."

I don't know if Daddy meant what he said to me. All I remember was that I was very angry. I did not like the new home; it was dirty and had no lights, the toilets were broken and the windows were all taped up with old newspaper. But the worst part was that the house was infested with nasty bedbugs (*wanzen*), and we had to sleep on the floor with the light on, because the pesky creepers would only come out and bite you and suck your blood when it was dark in the room.

During the day they were hiding under the base board and in cracks of the floor and the windows. Daddy used a torch and removed all the base boards and took care of all the bugs. He wanted to make sure that no more bugs or any other pests were living in our home, and after a few weeks we were all happy and bug free. Daddy also replaced the toilet and repaired all the walls.

During the war, every house was filled with alien soldiers from France, England, Italy, and Russia. Our house was the headquarters for the Russia soldiers. They had a very strange way to live. They all slept in their clothes and made sure no one could look through the windows by gluing newspaper on the glass. Dad told us the reason he had to replace the toilet bowls was also that the soldiers didn't know what a water toilet was because they had never seen one. Some soldiers tried to wash carrots and potatoes in the toilet, and when they pulled the string and flushed the water the food was gone, and the soldiers got mad because they thought the German people had used magic and put a spell on the toilet. They pulled the string again and again thinking the carrots and potatoes would come back, but no luck, so they took the gun and shot the toilet bowl. Jorg and I laughed when Daddy told us that.

Almost every house where the Russia soldiers lived needed new toilets and were bug infested. To make sure that all the homes were safe to live in and bug free, people had to call an exterminator for final inspection. When he came to our home, we had to leave for several hours, and Mother went shopping with us. She told us that Mr. Schmidt the exterminator would make sure we were able to sleep in the dark without being afraid that a bug would fall on our bed.

After a few hours, we returned to our home, and I'll never forget the terrible smell. I couldn't believe Mother. She told us when we left that we would have a nice home, but she never said that it would be stinky. The house was filled with smoke and every room had a penetrative smell. Yuck! It smelled awful. I was not surprised that all the bugs were gone because the smell would drive out even an elephant, I told Mr. Schmidt. He said, "I agree with you, smarty, but you will see; soon every room will smell like Christmas."

He brought a few evergreen branches and told Daddy to put them in a metal container and hold a lighted match to the green needles till they started to smoke, and the smoke would take care of the smell.

We were no longer sleeping on the floor, and Jorg and I had a room upstairs with a small window with red and blue curtains. When we took a chair, we could look out the window and watch cars, people, and animals crossing a big bridge. But the best part was to see the train going by directly in front of our house and disappearing in a long black tunnel. The steam was sometimes black, but most of the time it was white and thick.

Every time a train came out of the tunnel or went into the tunnel, the engine-driver blew the big horn. Mother tried to make it easy for us to get used to our new home, and I know it was not easy because we didn't have very much money and needed to get many things—like tables, oven, dishes, beds, chairs, and also food. Money was short, and we all learned very early to save things and use things carefully.

Mother knit, sewed, and crocheted, and Dad made all kinds of furniture. It didn't take him very long to fix things, and soon we had a very nice home.

We started to like it and when Daddy told us that Opa would soon come and visit us, I was more than happy. We would soon celebrate Christmas, and Opa would be with us. Jorg and I colored pictures for him, and I cut flowers out of paper. I helped mother to bake, and we made a Christstollen (a special German Christmas treat). We also made many cookies like macaroons, gingerbread nuts, anise stars, cinnamon stars, and marzipan. Jorg tried to help but mainly helped cleaning the leftovers of cream and sugar. His face was covered with cookie dough and almond and nut pieces.

I loved to help my mom. She was a very good cook and also had a great way to teach me. When I made a mess, I had to clean it up. In the beginning I had to clean a lot. In the evening we all gathered around a big table, and Mom put out some cookies and milk. Daddy had made a big *Adventskranz* (Advent wreath), and he hung it up with red bows on a stand. Between each bow he put a red candle, and we lit the first candle in the beginning of the Advent season four weeks before Christmas. After that, another candle, and when all four candles were lit, we knew that Christmas was not far away.

During the first week we also made all kinds of decorations for the Christmas tree. I made straw stars and stars cut out of very fine paper. I needed to help my brother to cut out stars. My daddy surprised us with a few Christmas records and an old record player, and we had a great time listening to the music. Dad had been gone for several hours, and when he finally came back, he had a long box and some small packages under his arm. He was acting very mysterious and went with Mom in the living room. The door was locked and a towel was hanging in front of the key hole to stop the curiosity of two little, nosy children. Jorg lay on his belly to look under the small opening but he was disappointed and said, "N-not f-f-fair!"

I start to laugh and he got mad at me. Mom came and told us that we all had to go pick up Opa, who would spend some time with us. Daddy said, "You are not allowed to open the door to the living room before you hear the bell ringing three times. By the way, you need to clean your room, and most of all you both need to be good and don't fight."

We promised to try to be good, but it wasn't easy because everything happening was so exiting, and my brother was not willing to do what I wanted to do.

Mother told us to get ready and put on boots, mittens, and a warm coat to pick up Opa from the train station. We had to walk about a half hour, and it was very cold. When we entered the station we could hear the train coming, and soon we heard the loud squeaky noise of the breaks as the conductor gave the stop sign. The engine driver stopped the train, and people came out of each railroad car.

I saw Opa and wanted to run, but Daddy held me back and said, "You stay right here, young lady. It is very dangerous for little girls, and Opa will be here soon. Remember, never run when a train has arrived because you don't know if another train is on its way. You see the railroad tracks? If you fall, a train can't stop immediately. This is why I told you both that you will get in trouble if I ever see you walking on the tracks in the back of our house."

Daddy was never very strict with me, but he was much stricter with my brother, sometimes maybe too strict, so Jorg was closer to mom; she let him get by with some things.

Opa walked up, and I forgot the lecture Daddy had given me. Opa gave me a hug and kiss and lifted me up in the air. I was happy and took Opa's hand. He gave Daddy a hug and kissed Mom, and we all left the station. Dad took care of Opa's suitcase, and soon we were on our way home. I was so happy and would not let go of Opa's hand. At home we all had a great evening meal, and soon it was time to go to bed because tomorrow would be Christmas—the first Christmas in our new home with my best, best, best Opa! Dad told us to put all the stars and decorations we made on the table by the Advent wreath so the angel would find them. Maybe we might get a little tree. I looked at Daddy and said, "Really? You mean a real tree, Daddy?"

Daddy smiled and said nothing. Opa also smiled and said nothing. I tried to get an answer from Mother, but she only said, "Okay, you both have talked enough, and it is time to go to bed. Christmas is a time for surprises, and you don't want to ruin a surprise by being so nosy."

Both Daddy and Opa agreed with Mom and left the room. Mom brought us some treats, gave us a kiss, and both Jorg and I went to bed. Opa and Daddy came and said goodnight and turned the light off. Soon the "Sandman" came with his magic sand and tossed it in the air. Jorg and I fell asleep after we prayed and talked to Jesus. I told Jesus that I couldn't wait to see him again tomorrow at church. Then I said, "I am sorry, Jesus, but I am so tired I will talk to you tomorrow. Thank You, dear Jesus, I love you. Goodnight. Amen!"

I think Jesus will always understand a child's prayer. Christmas was the next day!

The whole house was clean, and all our things we had scattered on the floor were picked up and put away. Opa, Mom, my brother, and I were waiting in the kitchen. We had to wait and listen to the sounds in the living room. "Where was Daddy?" I asked.

"He will be here soon," Opa said. "Just listen if you can hear the ringing of Christkindl's silver bell."

I tried very hard to listen, and all of the sudden Jorg shouted, "I h-h-heard the bell! I h-heard the bell! It s-s-said *ting*."

I also heard the soft tone and was getting very much exited. My Opa tried to calm me down and said, "Let's all be very quiet and listen if the bell will ring again, but this time it has to be two times."

We waited and there it was: *ting, ting* two times. One time more and we could enter the living room.

"Where is Daddy, Mom?" I asked again, and I looked at my mother.

She said, "Don't worry, Daddy will be here. Now listen if you can hear the bell ringing three times."

We moved closer to the door and Jorg took my hand. His big, blue eyes were wide open, and when the bell rang three times he was so surprised he was unable to open the door. Opa laughed and asked us why we didn't open the door.

Daddy said, "I could hear the ringing when I came in the kitchen."

I looked at Daddy and asked, "Where did you go, Daddy?"

He smiled and said, "I had to do something, but now let us open the door and see Christkindl's surprise."

Jorg was right by the door, and Opa helped him to push the door open. When the door was wide open, my brother was again not able to move, and this time his eyes and mouth were wide, wide open. But I also was amazed. A tall, beautiful tree was decorated with all the straw stars and paper stars Jorg and I had made, and many, many white candles were lit. There was also a manger under the tree, and in the manger was a baby smiling at my brother and me.

I whispered, "Jesus, I am so happy that You came to us."

Two wooden figures were also under the tree—Mary and Joseph. Before I could ask any questions, Daddy said, "I need to tell you the angels will be here next year because they had to fly to the church, and they know that you will be happy they have to make other children happy."

I said, "It is okay because Jesus is in our house."

We all sang: *Stille Nacht, Heilige Nacht* (Silent Night, Holy Night).

Daddy opened the Bible and read the Christmas story. Jorg and I had to say a little poem, and I sang a song. Jorg got stuck, and my tune was very much off, but I guess my parents didn't mind and got used to my singing. Opa had tears in his eyes when I sang (I thought maybe he couldn't hear my song so I sang very loudly).

Everyone clapped their hands. Only my brother said that I was awful, but Opa said, "You did good, baby. I like to hear you singing, but next time don't sing so loud."

Mother and Daddy pulled a white sheet away from the side and uncovered all the presents. We were speechless and couldn't move. What a surprise! Besides all kinds of clothes, there were also toys, books, and a big Christmas plate filled with cookies, candies, nuts, and fruit. Jorg got a wooden train with different railroad cars and a wooden farm house with pigs, cows, sheep, chickens, dogs and cats, and also a wooden tractor and little wooden people. I found a doll with real hair and a dress with little embroidered roses, and a beautiful doll house with a kitchen, a bedroom, a bath, and a play room with little furniture. It was a big house, and I had to get up on my tippy-toes to reach the roof.

Jorg and I gave Mom and Dad a picture we had colored, and I gave Opa a straw star and a big hug. Indeed it was a wonderful Christmas, and everyone was happy. The first Christmas after the war and the first Christmas in our new home with Daddy, Mom, my brother, and my Opa—it was unforgettable. I never forgot this time because my parents always found a way to surprise us every Christmas. Mom made doll clothes for my doll, and Dad made wooden toys for my brother. When I held the doll in my arm, Mom told me that I can comb her hair and change it because it was real hair and it was hair from my mom. She had a friend cut her hair short and used her long cut hair to make a wig for my new doll. I treasured this doll very much and was heartbroken when we moved and my doll broke. The doll was porcelain, and I never dropped her, but when we moved to another city my doll fell out of the box on the cement and broke in many pieces. I tried to glue the head and body together but the damage was too much and beyond repair. At that time, I was already a young adult, but it was not easy for me to put my doll in the trash can. I was also not able to save Mom's hair; it was full of porcelain pieces and glue.

We had a great time with Opa, and I think he also enjoyed being with us. When I didn't want to take a nap, Opa said, "I think I will lie down and we will both nap. I will tell you a story, and when I get tired, you will tell me a story. When we both get tired, we will both take a nap."

I agreed, and when naptime came, Opa and I went to his big bed and lay down. Opa started to tell me a fairy-tale story, and soon he started to snore. I left his room and told Mom, "You don't have to be worried, Mom. Opa was tired, and I could not finish my story. He is deep asleep."

Mom looked at me and said, "I don't know what it takes to have you take a nap. Well, I think when school starts next year you will be happy to take a nap."

When Opa woke up, he came in the kitchen, opened all the cabinet doors, looked in all the drawers, and called my name. Then he went to Mom and told her that he couldn't find me because when he woke up I was gone.

I started to giggle and called, "Opa, Opa, I am here! You are very funny. Why are you looking in the drawer? I can't fit in there."

Opa turned around and gave me a big hug and said, "Oh, I am so glad that I found you. I thought the big, fat wolf came and ate you."

We all laughed. Well, that was my naptime with Opa. I loved my Opa, and we always had a great time, but the very special time was when Opa took his little Bible and read story after story to me or when he told me about my grandma and how much he loved her. He also shared stories with me about when my mom was very young, and he often said that he never stopped trusting and loving Jesus, because without the guidance and love of Jesus Christ, he would have never been here and would have never become my Opa.

I must say that was very effective, and even when I was very young I began to reach out to Jesus when I felt lonely, lost, or in danger. Opa was the one and only person who made me believe, and when I look back, I can see his love, kindness, and understanding could only come from his belief in God and God's son, Jesus Christ the Lord.

Opa was also very concerned about my brother. Soon we had to go to school, and Jorg still had problems talking without stuttering. Opa would never lose patience; he always found a way to make us smile and be happy. Mom was very happy that Opa was living with us. Daddy worked for the railroad, and he had to leave sometimes in the middle of the night and take care of the luggage of people riding on the train. Daddy was often gone for several days, and most of the time on weekends he was a coach at football games.

I was not very much interested in any sport, and I know my dad was a little disappointed because my brother rather liked to draw pictures. When Jorg made a picture it was very good, but when I drew a picture I had to tell everyone what it was. Opa always loved my drawing. My dad only took me one time to the football game, and never again, because he was not very happy with my behavior. All the players were trying to do their best, and it was very quiet. One player tried to get the football, and others tried to stop him. I thought they were fighting over the ball, and I shouted as loud as I could, "Daddy, why don't you give them another ball because they fight over this ball?"

Of course everyone laughed and my dad was very embarrassed. Here he was a coach, and his daughter didn't know anything about football. But the coach's daughter was also the reason they lost the game.

5

February 1946: Teacher Learns a Lesson

It was February 1946, and school would start in March. Jorg and I had to go with Mother to a round-up for first graders. We had to walk over three hours, and I was very tired when we finally reached the school. Mother opened a very heavy, dark, oak door. We had to wait, and Mother gave us a little water because the long trip made us very thirsty. I asked Mom if we had to walk that long way every day. She looked at me and said, "Maybe, but I hope not, but we will see."

The door to the director's office opened, and a very nice older man told us to enter. He had dark glasses and carried in his hand several papers. Mom looked at him, and before she could say anything, the director told her not to worry because this school was not close enough for us to be enrolled. The law would not allow children to walk that far. The director looked at me and said, "You must be Alusru; that is a very nice name. Are you ready to go every day to school and to learn? Would you like to walk a shorter distance?"

I said, "I don't like to walk that long, and my brother doesn't like it either."

Mother smiled. The director gave her some papers to sign and told us that the Muehlendorf School was closer and we would be better off to be enrolled in there. Mother was glad because she knew that we would be unable to learn if we had to walk almost six hours every day to attend school.

The director told Mom that he would inform the school and let them know his reason, and the school would contact Mom to enroll us and let her know the time and the things we had to bring. He said goodbye to Mom and us, and apologized for the wrong information and that we had to walk such a long way without success.

We left and went back home. This was a long day, and Opa made us something to eat. After a short time, Mom took us to bed, tucked us into our blankets, kissed us, and turned the light off. Opa came and asked us if we would like to listen to a story, but we both said no; we were so tired! Opa smiled and we all prayed: "Dear Lord, thank You for all Your help and that we don't have to walk so far to school. Please, Lord, understand that I can't say any more because I am so tired. I am sorry, dear Jesus. Goodnight! Amen."

Opa said, "I know that Jesus will understand. Any time you have a problem, ask Jesus to help you. Now it is time to sleep. Tomorrow is not far away, and you both look very tired."

My eyes were very heavy, and soon I was sleeping and dreaming about the new school. Well, I hoped that we would have a nice teacher, that the school would not be very far, and that we would have a great time.

I was still tired when Mom came and told us to get ready to take a shower and eat breakfast because today was our first school day. We had to be at school by eight o'clock. I was still tired, and Jorg didn't want to get up, but Mom gave us no choice and Opa was also no help.

We finally got ready, and it was still dark when we left with Mother. We had to walk about five miles. The first three miles were easy because it was all the way on Main Street. The last two miles were going over the river bridge and up a steep hill, and soon we were standing in front of the school. Mother took us to the first grade class, and for the first time, Jorg and I were on our own because all parents had to leave the kids with the teacher.

All the kids tried to find a place to sit, and the teacher, a very young man, entered the classroom. He told us that his name was Mr. Young. He would be our teacher. He waited for the kids to be quiet, and he told us that he would try to do his best to make school a fun time, but we had to listen to him and follow his rules. Rule #1: When he was speaking, we had to listen. Rule #2: No fighting and pushing each other. Rule #3: Every kid has to be on time. Then he ordered everyone to step up front and take a seat he was assigning to each one of us. We had about eighty kids in our class, and on one side were the boys and on the other side, the girls. It took some time for all the kids to be seated.

Mr. Young asked everyone to say their first name, and he wrote each name on a sticky paper. Each kid had to put the sticky name tag on the front of his or her desk. This was our first assignment, and we had to learn and memorize all the names. The day went by very fast, and after three hours we were allowed to go home. Mother was outside to meet us.

The school director handed each kid a cone-shaped paper bag filled with paper, pencils, and some candies and fruit. He told us that he was very happy to see so many children in his school, and he promised to do everything to help us to become good students and to learn everything we needed to be successful in the future.

Before we could leave, we had to pray and ask the Lord for His guidance and protection. Jorg and I were happy to see Mother, and soon we were all on our way home. Opa was waiting for us, and he also had a big cone paper bag for Jorg and me, filled with all kinds of goodies. He gave us both a big "elephant" hug and told us soon we would be so smart that we would need to teach him because it was a long time since he went to school to learn. Now we will learn all the new things. Opa smiled, looked at me, and said, "But one thing will always be the same, and that is math (*rechnen*). It will never change, and 1+1 will always be 2, and 2+2 will always be 4; this will never change. When you learn the basics, you will have no problems to solve and understand numbers and problems."

I looked at Opa and said, "I will always ask Jesus if I have a problem. Opa, did Jesus go to school and have to learn all the numbers and letters like we have to learn?"

Opa took me on his lap and laughed. He said, "You, little smarty, have many questions, but this question I can't answer, because I don't know the answer. I only know that Jesus was a teacher very early, and he was teaching God's word, telling people to love one another and to share and help. I think that this was much more important than any numbers or letters. Besides Jesus is God's son. And all things come from God. I believe that Jesus had all knowledge to teach and to be a good teacher. So if you have a question and I can't answer you, all I can say is ask Jesus, and He will give you the right answer. It is written in God's book: *Ask and it shall be given to you! Seek and you shall find! Knock and it shall be opened unto you.* This is written in God's book the Bible, and Jesus said this to everyone when He was teaching and when He was preaching. It is written in Matthew 7:7 and Luke11:9. I also need to tell you that it is very important to listen to your teacher in the school, and if you have questions and don't understand, you need to ask your teacher. He or she is able to answer and to help. This is why they have the title of teacher. Not everyone will be a good teacher, but you both are little students, and a student needs to be willing to learn and to study."

Opa always told me there is nothing in this world that a person can't learn. With God all things are possible, and if we are willing to learn, we can have all kinds of knowledge, and soon learning will be fun. Every day we will discover new things and understand more and more. But right now, everything is very difficult to understand, and we would rather play than learn to write and read.

"Okay, now I have told you both all kinds of things about learning, and I hope you will have lots of fun, but now it is time to stop and don't worry about school."

Mom had supper ready, and after we ate, we helped her with the dishes. Then we all sat down and played a board game. Opa tried to let us win many times and pretended to be angry when he lost. We always had a great time when we played *Mensch aergere Dich nicht* (something like Sorry!). We also had many different card games, and the whole family sat down and played. We learned soon to win and to lose. After several games, it was time to take a bath and get to bed because soon would be tomorrow, and we had to get up early. A new chapter in our life began tomorrow. It was our first school day—*our first day without Mom, Dad, and Opa!*

I fell asleep after I prayed with Opa. I asked Jesus to help me and to help Jorg tomorrow—and every day—in school. Today, I have to say I knew without the guidance and great love of Jesus Christ, I would never be here today, and many things would have gone very wrong. I am very thankful for all the time I was able to spend with Opa.

When Mom came and woke us up, Jorg and I were still tired, but soon we were on our way to school. We all had to line up at the school yard, and the teacher guided us to the classroom—one line the girls and one line the boys. No one was allowed to talk. I still remember the long hallway and the many doors on both sides. Behind each door was a big classroom, and over the door was a black number. A huge staircase led to the second floor, and across the stairs were two big windows. This was the office of the *rektor* (principal) and his two secretaries. Everyone who came to the school had to walk by the office, and if school was already started, they had to stop at the office. If the student came late, he or she had to report to the principal, and the secretary took the student to the classroom. Every student needed to be on time, and if we were several times tardy we had to stay longer after school or our parents were called in for a special meeting. It was called the tardiness student meeting.

In the beginning of the new school year, many parents had to attend the meeting, and some weren't happy when they were called the second time, or better, when they received a letter from the school more than once. Every three months the school called for a parent/teacher meeting, and tardiness was number one on the agenda.

When my parents had to come in for a meeting the first time, we both got in trouble, and my dad was upset with us. We had to get up thirty minutes earlier, and all our things needed to be ready before we went to bed. School was a very important time. When we came home, we were often very tired because it was such a long walk, and we had to carry all our books and paper. In the first year, we learned to write and to behave. We didn't have paper and pens or pencil because all first graders learned writing on a slate using a special slate pencil (*griffel*). I can't remember how many times my parents had to replace my slate, because when we dropped it on the floor it cracked.

Mom made many slate rags, and I learned very early to knit and crochet, because every day we had to have a clean slate rag (*tafel-lappen*). I know my brother needed a new slate more often because he was not very careful and dropped his school bag (*tornister*) many times. I think if Opa wasn't with us Jorg would be in much more trouble because Dad would discipline him every time for a cracked slate. Opa often protected us when Dad was ready to spank us.

Sometimes Opa took us to town and bought us a new slate or slate pencil. When we asked him for a treat he used his little blue Bible and said, "Let's see what Jesus would do," and soon we were both happy because Opa gave us one *mark* (dollar) or bought us a treat. Sometimes he had to get back to Bochum, and Jorg and I missed him every day. But there were many times when Opa visited us, and this was always a great surprise.

Our first school year was almost over, and we were given a new teacher because Mr. Young had to leave us. His replacement, Mrs. Langenfeld, was a very old lady, and she would be our teacher for one more year. I remember that she sometimes sat at her desk snoring. We didn't dare to wake her up because it was more fun to see her sleeping than to hear her yelling at us. Mrs. Langenfeld gave every student a good score who came to school and brought her bones for her two dogs.

She was not a bad teacher, but she was very old and had very little understanding of little unruly kids. One day she was sick, and we had another teacher, Mr. Brown. He had to teach another class at the same time, and he gave us some work to write and some math to solve. He told us that he would leave the door open and anyone who talked would be in trouble and he would spank. I told Jorg to do his work, and I was doing my work.

As soon as Mr. Brown left, most of the kids began to laugh and talk. When the teacher came back, he asked who started the trouble, and one boy shouted, "Jorg did!"

The teacher pulled my brother out of his seat in front of the class and reached for the wooden stick to spank him. I was so angry I jumped out my seat, took all my stuff from my desk, threw it at the teacher, took my brother and ran with him down the hall. I shouted, "I don't like to go to the school when the teacher is unfair. My brother didn't do it!"

Jorg was very surprised but also happy that he didn't get a spanking. Before we reached the front door, we were stopped by Mr. Holt, the principal. He took us into his office, and before he stepped behind his desk, I shouted at him and told him that I would not come back to school if Mr. Brown was our teacher because he was unfair and would spank kids without any reason.

Mr. Holt smiled at me and said, "Alusru, you need to tell me what are you talking about, and I will see if I can talk to the teacher."

I tried to tell the principal everything, saying, "You see, the boy didn't like Jorg, and he said my brother started the trouble because he knew that my brother can't explain things because he gets very upset when he has to talk, and he stutters. Then all the kids laugh, so he'd rather not talk. He is my brother, and I have to help and protect him because I love him."

I looked at the principal and began to cry. Mr. Holt was not angry, and he told me to stay at his office and not to be afraid because he would talk to the teacher. Jorg and I sat down, and I asked Jesus to help make the teacher better.

I think Jesus went to work right away because when Mr. Brown entered the office he was not angry. He looked at me, gave me a big hug, and said, "Alusru, I am so sorry that I was so upset. I was very wrong, and you are a very good sister. Jorg, you can be very proud to have such a caring sister. I have to apologize to both of you. Let's be friends and go back to the classroom."

I looked at the teacher and said, "I think Jesus took care of us; let's go back. Thank You, Jesus."

I think both the teacher and principal were very surprised by my answers and reactions. They both had tears in their eyes, and the teacher took Jorg's hand and walked with us back to the classroom. All the kids looked at us and wanted to find out what the principal said to us and if Jorg got a spanking.

Mr. Brown took me in front of the class and said, "You all have to apologize to Alusru and Jorg because you all blamed Jorg knowing that he would not defend himself. You all thought it would be okay if he got spanked, and I almost spanked an innocent boy because I believed you all. But today I learned something I never will forget, and I took a lesson from a little seven-year-old girl. She threw pens and books at me and protected her brother. Alusru is a very brave girl, and she is not afraid to fight for her brother. She is willing to get herself in trouble if she can help Jorg. I think Alusru should tell me what I should do to all of you."

The kids looked at me, and some were afraid; some faces turned red. It was very quiet. I smiled and answered, "I think it is okay, Mr. Brown. I don't think they will do it again."

Almost everyone smiled, and Mr. Brown said, "I think Alusru is also a good judge. She would be a great candidate for becoming a class speaker."

Everyone clapped their hands, and my face turned red when I went back to my seat. I didn't know that Mr. Brown was on the right track. Two years later I became class speaker, and any time we had a problem or a request, the class came to me and I picked a few other kids to form a group to talk things over. After we reached an agreement, I went to the teacher and explained the situation or request.

I didn't have many problems to talk to the teacher about, and most of the time I received an okay. Everyone was happy and satisfied.

Sometimes I was very surprised that the teacher said okay to our request. But I think it was Jesus who told the teacher what to say, because every time I asked Jesus to help me when I had to talk to the teacher. Mr. Brown became our teacher for three years, and I have to say he was a great teacher. We had over ninety students in our class, and school time was very important.

6

Surprise Message from Mom, Dad, and Opa

Now, I will tell you more about my school years, and I will focus on special things.

Jorg and I tried very hard to be on time, and if we were late we took a shortcut, but it was a risk because if Dad found out, we would be in trouble.

One morning Jorg and I woke up very late and we needed to be in school by eight, so I told my brother we would take a shortcut. Dad wasn't home, and I made Jorg promise me not to say anything to Dad. We both were in third grade, and it was late. I decided to walk over the bridge on the tracks. Instead of walking the long way on Main Street, we went down the river passing by the junk dealer. We had to cross the tracks on the other side of the junk yard. I made sure that old Theo wouldn't see us. We were lucky Theo was not there, and we made it to the bridge. I told Jorg to walk fast. I was a little afraid, and my heart was pounding in my chest. So I started to pray: "Oh, Jesus, we know that we are not allowed to walk on the tracks, but, Jesus, You know it is a shorter way to school, and You know that we are late. Please, Jesus, don't tell Daddy, and please, Jesus, forgive us because we are doing something wrong. Jesus, this is Alusru and Jorg. We love you. Please, Jesus, let the bridge be open on the end. Thank you!"

But the bridge was not open, and we had to climb over the iron fence. Jorg tried to tell me that God didn't hear me because the bridge was closed, but I told him Jesus forgot the keys, but He helped us because we made it on time before a train came. I said, "You know that it was your fault that we were late because you couldn't get out of your bed. Promise me that you will never do it again."

Before we reached the school, I said, "Thank You, Jesus, for helping us, and it is okay that you forgot the keys to the bridge. Jorg and I promise You to be good; we only went this way because we were late." Today, I have to say that we used the shortcut many times and Dad never found out.

We also used another shortcut, and we had to cross the river. It was a great shortcut but also very dangerous because we had to walk through the riverbed when the water was controlled by the city and ran into another riverbed. A big cement wall divided the two riverbeds. Many students used this shortcut, and some even went through the river walking on the slippery stones. We always took a chance when we went over the *wehr*. Sometimes we could see from the street if the river was safe because the water wasn't moving. We also had several accidents, and kids fell in the river when crossing the cement wall. Many times I lost my shoes and socks. Most times we used this shortcut on the way home.

During the winter time, almost every kid living on the other side of the river used the riverway, but it was always a risk. Jorg never had a problem because he could walk over the wall like walking on the street. I was always scared to walk, and I had to hold on to my brother. This was a reason for him to call me a scaredy-cat; some words he couldn't say, but scaredy-cat was easy for him, and he enjoyed it. But I loved him anyway and helped him when he needed my help.

Soon we would be in fourth grade, and some of our classes changed. The girls had to learn sewing, knitting, crocheting, cooking, and raising children. The boys had to learn mechanics, woodwork, algebra, and high business math.

I had no problem to knit, sew, or crochet. My mom had taught me all the basics when I was very young, but cooking and raising a family was something I had to learn. I had helped my Mom when she made a meal, but I had to learn more to become a good cook. When we were asked to hold a baby doll like a real baby, I was not very talented, and several times I dropped the baby. When I told my mom that I had to learn how to take care of a baby, her face turned red and she smiled at me. She told me that she had a surprise for me, but she wanted to wait until Opa came to visit us; he would be staying for a while.

I was so excited to hear that my Opa was coming to visit us again. But why did Mom have to wait to tell me more about cooking and holding a baby? I wanted to ask her, but I chose not to and later forgot it.

I went to see Jorg, but he was not in his room, so I went outside. Dad was still working and would be home soon. It was late, and Jorg was still outside. Mom had made a special supper and had called him several times. A train was coming and Jorg was not home. Where was he? The train was very close, and Mom was worried; just two weeks ago Mr. Eisen, a very close neighbor, was killed right in front of our house. It was terrible; he was such a great person and left behind five little children who had to grow up without a daddy. Mrs. Eisen is still in shock, and Mom is very concerned about her, so she helps her whenever she can. Soon she will help her to pack all her belongings because Mrs. Eisen will move with her children to a home in the country. Her brother and sister will take care of her, and they will live on a small river with no train going close by.

Mom went again to the window to call Jorg. The train was coming, and I ran to the window. I was so excited when I saw Daddy waving at me. I shouted loudly, "Mommie, I saw Daddy! He is coming home!"

I was happy and jumped up and down. I forgot all about my brother, and just before I could reach the door, the door flew open and Jorg rushed in. His face was dirty, and his clothes were wet. What was wrong? Mom looked up and asked Jorg what happened, why his pants and shirt were wet, and why he didn't answer when she called. Jorg didn't answer, so Mom told him to change and to clean up before Daddy came.

Jorg went to his room, and I could see that he was very upset. I tried to talk to him, but he started to cry and said over and over again, "B-B-Bobby, Bobby is g-g-gone. He was there but h-he is g-g-gone. I tried to h-h-help, but I couldn't h-hold on. He is gone. My b-b-best friend is gone, Alusru. Theo tried too."

I had a very bad feeling, and I went to Mom and tried to tell her, but she could not talk to me because Daddy came with two policemen and told me to call Jorg. My brother was afraid and tried to hide under his bed. The policemen went to our room and told him not to be afraid. All they wanted was to talk to him. Dad and I went downstairs and Mom started to cry. I didn't know what was wrong, but when Dad told me that Bobby fell in the river, and they couldn't find him, I also cried because he is Jorg's and my friend.

The policemen came with Jorg and told Daddy that all the kids who played by the river had said the same thing—that Bobby tried to walk in the water and slipped and fell. Jorg tried to pull Bobby, but he was not able to hold on to him, and Bobby went under the water.

The policemen told Jorg that he shouldn't play by the river because the river is dangerous, and soon the city will close the levee and embankment, and the children will have new playgrounds in several areas without any danger. But the police also told Daddy that Jorg was a very brave boy because he had tried to pull Bobby out, and also went to call Theo.

I remember that day, and I will never forget when they found Bobby's body on the other side of the river. It was very sad, and Bobby's mom cried, and Bobby's sister Helga screamed. Everyone was sad.

Well, these are things no one can forget, and they have an effect on every life. My brother had a very difficult time understanding, and I had to keep him close to my side, because every time he wanted to go to the river, Mom was afraid he would drown. I promised her to watch.

When Helga and I became very good friends, she also helped Jorg to let it go. It also helped when Opa came to stay with us for a few months. Daddy, Jorg, and I went to the train station to pick him up. I was so happy to be with Opa again, and I had a hard time waiting for the train.

Jorg found a bench and sat down. I heard the train entering the big hall. The steam filled up the station, and the locomotive made a loud noise. The engine driver blew the whistle and brought the train to a hold. Now we had to wait for all the people to come. I saw Opa and I wanted to run, but Dad held me back and told me to wait. Opa was finally here, and nothing could be wrong anymore.

He gave Dad a big hug, and Dad said, "The kids don't know, Papa" (Mom and Dad called Opa Papa). Opa smiled, and I tried to find out what Daddy was saying. What was it we didn't know? I asked Daddy, but he said, "You will find out soon enough, so don't ask. Just wait and be patient."

Dad told Opa about the bad accident of Mr. Eisen and the tragedy of Bobby's drowning death. Opa gave Jorg a big hug and said, "I am so proud of you that you tried to rescue your friend, but I think Bobby is with Jesus, and he is very happy that you are his friend. He will watch over you so you don't fall in the river, but you need to promise me that you will not go to the river alone anymore."

Jorg took Opa's hand and said, "I p-promise."

We had reached our home, and Mom gave Opa a kiss and said, "The kids don't know, Papa."

Here was it again. What was it that we didn't know? Because we were the only kids, Jorg and I. I know I could not ask again because Dad said be patient, so I started to focus on Opa. Maybe he would tell me. So I decided to try to have patience, and maybe if I had a moment without the watch of Mom and Dad, I might have a chance to ask Opa. Obviously he knew the big secret and he would tell me, but I was wrong; when I had the chance to ask Opa he said, "Oh no, your mom and your dad will tell you early enough; I will not spoil the surprise for you. So, my dear, nosy girl, have patience."

Jorg said, "I know, Alusru, w-we will get a p-p-puppy."

Opa started to laugh, and I told Jorg, "I think you are wrong. I think maybe we will move because Mom is so afraid that you will get hurt on the railroad tracks or in the river."

Opa said, "You both can say what you want; I will not tell what the big surprise is. So just wait until your mom and dad tell you."

Opa was always great, and I loved him so much, but he also taught me to listen. And when he said *no*, he would not change to *yes*. This is one of the reasons why I loved my Opa so much—because he was always open and straight and explained things in a way I could understand.

Mom came in, looked at Opa, and said, "Let's all sit down, and Dad and I will tell you the wonderful news."

Opa took my hand and told Mom that he thought it was a good idea to tell the great and wonderful news. I looked at Mom and said, "Jorg said we will get a puppy or a little kitty. Is Jorg right, Mom?"

"Well," Mom said, "not quite right, but close. You see, God will give us another baby, and you will have another brother or a little sister. It is all up to God; if He wants you to have a sister you will have a sister, but if He decides to bless us with another little boy, you will soon have another little brother to love and to teach. We don't know what God has planned under my heart because this is God's surprise, and I will carry this new baby under my heart. When the time comes that it gets too big, God will help me and open a door for the baby to be born, and then you can hold and kiss your new sister or brother. Mom will need you to be very good and to help because when the baby gets bigger, Mom will not be able to do all the things she did before. I will always love you both, and I know you both will be a wonderful brother and sister to the new baby. Now you know, Alusru, why I didn't say much when you told me about your new class in housekeeping and raising a family; you will learn all the things soon with me when the baby is here."

Mom looked at me and smiled. She took my hand and put it on her stomach and told me to push my hand against it and try to hold still for a while. I was so excited, and I could feel something kicking my hand. I said, "She kicked me, Mom! My sister kicked my hand."

Jorg wanted to feel the baby, too, and said, "No, that was not a sister; that was a brother. A girl cannot kick like that."

I was very upset, but Mom said, "Alusru, I told you we don't know what God has placed under my heart, and we need to accept His decision. God knows what is best for us. You will be a good sister regardless what."

Well, I was not so sure, and Daddy told me to put sugar out because sometimes a stork would come and exchange the baby. I made sure that I never forgot to put sugar out, and I told the Stork not to bring a boy. Opa tried to change my mind in case the stork had only boys in his nest, but nothing helped, and I was not willing to talk. I already had a name for the baby. Every time Mom let me put my hand on her stomach, I could feel the kick and said, "It is okay, Susie, your sister will teach you how to kick. Jorg is wrong. You will be a girl."

I told the baby that I also put sugar out in case God had made a mistake and put the wrong baby under Mom's heart. Mom, Dad and Opa gave up on me, and Jorg only smiled at me. I was sure that I would soon have a sister.

The day was close for the baby, and God opened the door and put the baby in Mom's arms. Daddy called us to greet the baby, and Opa took my hand and told me, "Alusru, God gave you a sweet little baby brother."

I cried and didn't want to see the baby. A lady, the midwife, came and told me, "You have a little brother, and he is so sweet."

I was angry and I asked her, "If he is so sweet, why don't you take him and exchange him for Susie? Don't you know that I already have a brother? I know God made a mistake, and He wouldn't mind giving the boy to a family who wants a boy. We want a girl."

The lady laughed and said, "I think you will love your brother, and by the way, God never makes a mistake."

Opa agreed with the lady and put his arm around me. He said, "Let's go, little princess, and greet the new little brother. You will see, you will soon love him very much."

I was not so sure, but I finally went to look at my new brother. I told Mom Jorg was right, and now we have two boys. I touched my new little brother's hand and wanted to see his eyes, but Mom said he was tired because he had a long way to come.

"Mom, can we call him George?" I asked.

Mom said she thought it was a nice name and she would ask Daddy.

The baby was sucking on his little finger and soon started to cry. Opa said, "Let the little George be with Mom and sleep because Mom and your brother are tired."

We both left the room. Jorg came and said, "I-I t-t-told Daddy to c-c-call my brother Heinz and Daddy s-said okay."

Opa took Jorg on the side and told him to let Mom and Dad decide and not to get angry at each other. "You both should be very happy that you have such a wonderful, healthy, little brother, and there is no reason to fight."

When Daddy's sister came to see the baby, she said, "Alusru, I thought you wanted a little sister. Didn't Dad tell you to put sugar out for the stork?"

I told her that I did it, and that the old stork took the sugar but he didn't have any girls left.

My aunt laughed and said, "Did you put only brown sugar out? Because if you wanted a sister you needed to put only brown sugar out."

I said, "No, Daddy said only sugar. You think I could have a sister if I had put brown sugar out?"

Dad came and he said, "That is enough. You have a brother, and we will call him George."

Well at least Jorg wasn't right when he called the baby Heinz. I had to get used to the fact that I was now a sister to two brothers.

My mom needed much help, and I learned finally how to hold a baby without dropping it. It was not easy. George also was not very cooperative because he moved and kicked all the time, and screamed when I tried to hold him tight. But soon I had no more problems, and I helped Mom to give George a bath and to change his diapers. Every time I was dressing him, I dressed him like a girl, and I was surprised that he smiled at me and giggled.

My brother Jorg was not very happy when he saw George was wearing a dress and had bows in his hair. He looked at George and said, "He l-looks so s-s-silly, and I d-don't think he is v-v-very happy."

Dad didn't say very much, and Mom only smiled. So in my mind, it was okay to dress my brother this way. It helped me a lot to forget that I wanted a sister.

Opa tried many times to tell me how great it was that we had another brother and that God had made the right decision to bless our family with such a beautiful boy. I was not so sure and I said, "But, Opa, didn't you say that God answers our prayers and gives us what we ask for? I prayed and asked Him to give me a sister, but God gave me a brother. Why?"

Opa looked at me and said, "Alusru, God will always answer your prayer, and He knows what everyone needs. He decides how to answer every prayer, and God never makes a mistake. You asked God to give you a sister, and your brother asked God to give him a brother. God answered your brother's request because God knew that you are a good little girl and that you can handle a little disappointment better than your brother, so God gave your mom, your dad, your brother, and you a healthy boy. I can see that you love your brother, and that is the most important part in a family—to love and teach and help each other. I know you love Jorg, and you helped him a lot to learn to speak. You have a lot of patience to teach him to speak, and Jorg loves you very much, which is a wonderful sister-brother relationship. So now you need to give the same love to your new baby brother George. I also know that your mom and dad will be very happy when you tell them that it is good that you have another brother. Promise me that you will at least try to accept God's answer."

I remember that Opa had tears in his eyes when he talked to me. Then he said something I never forgot. He told me that I was always his special little princess and that I was his baby. "Alusru, it makes no difference that I am only your stepgrandpa. I will always love you all the same, and when you become a grandma, you must remember it doesn't matter if your grandchildren are your own flesh and blood or if your son or daughter married a man or woman with children. Never ever make a difference, because when a child loves you, you need to love that child also. This is so important; a child who is being loved by Grandpa and loved by Grandma will always reach out for more love and will grow up to become a good mom or dad.

"You see, your mom didn't know her real dad because he never came back from the war, and when I met your grandma, God told me to take her in my arms and take care of her children. I took over, and your mom loved me from the very first moment and accepted me as her new daddy. She called me Papa. I love your mom very much, and I also love her brother, but I wish I would have done a better job with your mom's brother because he is very well known and very successful but has never learned the most important things in God's teaching. It makes no difference who you are; never look down on others.

"Your mom and her brother never had a very deep relationship with each other, and this is partly my fault because I could have guided him in a better way. I focused all my love on your grandma because she was often very sick, and I let things go by when I should have be a father to your uncle. Your uncle was also very sick when he was still in school. He was in the hospital for almost a year with rheumatic fever. During this time he was most of the time all by himself because I had to take care of your mom and your grandma. You know that your grandma died very young, and Albert was very close to his mom. It was a shock for him to lose his mom, but he never gave up on learning. You know that he is a pastor and has committed his life to preach God's word. This is a promise he had made to his mom. To this day, he has kept his promise, and, you know, when he preaches the church is packed, and his preaching is very powerful. But we need to pray for him, and we need to ask God to put more love and kindness in his life and in his words. Only God can soften his mind and heart.

"Well I think I have said enough, and I know God can do anything."

I put my arms around Opa's neck and gave him a kiss. "Opa, I love you so much, and I promise you to be a good sister to my brothers. But you have to promise me that you will be with us more often, and when you have to go to Bochum you will tell Uncle Albert that I do love him and Aunt Hanna."

Jorg came in and said, "Alusru, w-we are going t-to the r-r-river t-t-tomorrow. O-Opa is cutting s-s-sticks."

I looked at Opa, and he made a very guilty face and said, "Oh, I am so sorry. I forgot all the news, can you forgive me little baby? Yes, I will take you both to the river, and you can play in the water by the shore when I cut some sticks for the tomatoes, peas, and beans. The plants in the garden need to get some support, and brushwood and sticks are the best to cut by the river. But you both need to promise me not to walk into the river and not to walk away where I can't see you."

We were very excited and told Opa that we would be good. Mom called us for supper, and Opa reminded us to wash our hands. We all sat down and Mom asked Opa to pray. I still remember when Opa prayed, and I will never forget the words he used in all his prayers. He always started his prayers with a word of praise and thanks for all the things God had done, and then he put each one of us in the Lord's hand. But all of his prayers he closed with one powerful trust sentence: *Lord, not my will, only Your will be done, I pray to You in Your Holy and wonderful name, Jesus Christ! Amen.*

When I close my eyes I still can see and hear my Opa, and I have many times used the same words. Sometimes it was very difficult to close my prayer with the words, *Lord, not my will, only Your will be done!* But most of the time I was amazed how the Lord answered. I am so thankful for Opa.

After supper we helped with the dishes, and I helped Mom to take care of my baby brother. Soon it was time to go to bed. I was tired, and Jorg and I fell asleep.

The next day we were ready to go with Opa to the river. Opa started to cut some brushwood and sticks. Jorg and I played by the river and were surprised when we saw some kids walking by the river. Jorg was friends with two boys and wanted to walk with the kids up the hill to the mountain cliff. I decided to go with them, and when we looked at Opa, we saw that he was very busy. I shouted, "Opa, we are going with the kids to pick some blueberries."

Opa looked up and said, "Alusru, don't go too far. I am almost ready, and don't climb the mountain cliff."

I think these were the last words I remember. When we ran up the hill, I had a very difficult time to keep up with the others, but I refused to turn back, so I climbed the mountain cliff also. I totally ignored Opa and had a very difficult time breathing. My heart was pounding, and soon I felt dizzy. I tried to tell my brother that I couldn't climb anymore, but Jorg laughed and told me to go back.

He went with the kids, and soon I couldn't see anyone. I was scared and decided to go back to Opa. I called Opa but didn't get any answer, so I started to go back. My feet were sore and, I got lost. I didn't know which way to go. When I started to turn, I lost my balance and fell down. I tried to hold on to a rock, but I couldn't, and began to slide and roll down the mountain cliff. I don't know how long it took because I can't remember. All I remember is that I saw a little tree and I was hoping that I could hold on to the tree, and maybe I was close to Opa. I knew I would be in trouble, but Opa would eventually forgive me.

I stopped sliding and reached for the tree, but when I felt the tree moving, I called Jesus. Then I saw the river and knew soon I would be falling down, and it was a long way down. I wished I would have listened to Opa. The little tree could not hold me anymore, and I passed out. I started to fall down. No one could save me because the cliff was solid rocks, but God heard Opa's cry and sent an angel to catch my body and carry me to a soft spot between the rocks and the trees.

Opa told me later that he almost got hit by falling rocks and was not very happy because he would have gotten hurt. When he looked up to tell us not to throw rocks, he saw my body and the tree. He knew if I would fall I would not survive. He called out to Jesus and begged him to save me. In his words, he went on his knees and pleaded to the Lord, "Please, Lord, save my baby. I know You can, but not my will, Your will be done."

Opa also told me that he saw two mighty hands catching my body and carrying me ten feet, if not more, to a soft spot just big enough for a child. Opa climbed over big rocks to reach my body. He was afraid that I was badly hurt, and when he saw me, he cried and fell on his knees. I can't count how many times Opa told us that he felt the presence of the Lord when he lifted me up and carried me home.

He held me close and thanked the Lord over and over. My mom cried and I woke up. Opa put me on the couch, and then he left. He was afraid that Jorg was also lost in the mountain cliff. He went to find him. When he reached the river, he saw many people, and he thought that Jorg or the other kids had fallen off the cliff. But when he turned around, he saw Jorg, and Jorg asked Opa where I was because the people were looking for my body. They saw it from the other side of the river. They called the police, and everyone was looking.

Opa told the police that I was okay and, yes, I had fallen down the mountain cliff, but I was okay because my body landed on a very soft spot. The police officer went up the big mountain cliff, and when the officer came back he told everyone that he had no explanation how I could have been okay and survived the fall from the mountain cliff, which was about two hundred and fifty feet down. Besides, if I had fallen down straight, my body would be shattered.

A young man said, "Officer, I saw it, and I can prove it because if you get up higher you will see the place where the little girl fell and rolled all the way to the cliff."

He pointed up to the top and said, "You see? The tree is gone. I think if the tree was still there, the little girl would be okay."

Opa went to the spot where the angel had put my body and told everyone that I was alive and that God had saved me. Many people could not believe it and came to our house to see for themselves and to talk to me. My mom had called Doctor Becker from a railroad control office, which was across from our house, to make sure that I was okay. Opa came home with Jorg and two police officers when Doctor Becker arrived.

He was a very kind and wise doctor. He loved children, and when he saw me, he smiled and said, "Alusru, Alusru, you must be very special to God, because when He sends His angels to save a little girl who didn't listen to her grandpa, that is something great. I only need to check you to make sure that you are okay."

Doctor Becker asked me to move my head and to lift my arms and legs. I said nothing was hurting; I only had a headache. He put some bandages over the scrape wounds and ordered an ice pack for my head. I was also not allowed to run around or get out of the bed.

Opa came, and I started to cry; I felt very guilty and asked Opa to forgive me and not to be mad because I didn't listen to him. I knew I made him so scared.

Opa couldn't stop crying, and he put his big arms all around me and said, "Oh, my baby, my sweet little princess, I am so happy that God has saved you. I saw the mighty hands of an angel holding you and carrying you to safety. I felt Jesus, and I know God heard my cry and sent His angels. I do believe if you follow the Lord—honor, worship, and obey Him—God has a plan for you, and He will always be with you and answer your prayers in His way. You are a little child, and when God uses a child to let people feel His mighty power, it is always a great and wonderful miracle.

"Alrusu, you need to believe, and you need to listen to God and follow Jesus Christ. Never, ever, try to question God's work and answers. Anything that comes from God is good. People will always try to tell you different and will even make fun of you when you tell them about Jesus, and they will laugh at you, but if you do what God told you to do and ignore all the others, God will be with you wherever you go. But now you need to get some rest, and tomorrow you will have to answer some questions. The police need to fill out a report, and the newspaper also has some questions for you."

Opa gave me a kiss and left my room. I was very tired and my head was hurting, but soon I fell asleep and slept until next morning.

Doctor Becker came and gave me another checkup. He was satisfied and gave Mom some instructions, but before he left he told me to stay in my bed and keep the ice on my head. Later the police came, and a lady from the newspaper. She asked me all kinds of questions, and I told her that I remembered falling, rolling, sliding down, and stopping at a little tree. I saw the river and the rocks, and I called Jesus. Then I woke up in Opa's arms carrying me home. I told the same to the police when they tried to confuse me. I said, "Jesus helped me, and you can see I am okay. All I have is a headache. I know that Jesus came and saved me."

When they tried to ask my brother Jorg, he didn't have any problem talking and told them he felt bad that he went up the mountain cliff because it was very difficult. He should have listened to Opa and stayed with me by the river. Besides, he was older and should have helped me.

Finally the people left and the newspaper printed an article about the mountain cliff and the miracle the next day. But many people didn't believe it, and when my mom went to the store, she heard people talking about it. One lady told another about this terrible accident and that the police found the body of that little girl totally crushed. They kept going on and on and started to tell each other how much they felt sorry for the mother because it was her only child.

Mom went to the ladies and thanked them for feeling sorry for the poor mother, but she also set the record straight and told the ladies that I was fine, and they should be telling everyone that the little girl is not hurt because God saved her.

When Mom came home, she was very much upset because she couldn't believe how fast the people start to tell false stories and turn the truth into rumors. It can hurt people and ruin their life. Opa tried to talk to her. He told her that this is life, and as long as we all tell the truth, do not repeat people's rumors, and trust the Lord, God will bless us and watch over us. He will also give us peace in our hearts and in our minds.

Mom smiled and said, "Oh, Papa, what would I do if I didn't have you? I am so thankful that God gave me you to be my papa." I know Mom loved Opa very much, and it was always very hard for all of us when Opa had to leave for a few months. But he promised always that he would come back soon.

Now was the time to say goodbye, and it was not easy because he is a member of our family. I knew I would miss him very much. I wanted to be strong when Opa left, but I couldn't stop crying. I didn't want to say goodbye.

George said, "Bye, bye, Opa." He didn't cry, and he giggled when I picked him up.

Mom also had tears in her eyes, and when I asked her, she said that she needed to go to the bathroom and didn't have time, so God helped moms when they had to go and didn't have time.

I thought that was very nice that God did that, and the only question I had was whether I could do the same or if I had to become a mom first. I really didn't like to go to the bathroom when I was busy.

Mom looked at me and said, "This is only for a mom because God knows that moms are very busy."

I didn't ask any more questions, but I decided never to forget this, and when I would become a mom, I would say the same to my kids.

7

Who Is Mr. Allen?

Daddy came home and told us that we would soon have some company; a very good friend from his school would come and visit us, so we needed to be very good because he didn't like any naughty kids. I said, "I don't think I will like him, because all kids are sometimes naughty. Opa said that Jesus loves me even when I am a naughty kid."

Daddy looked at me and said, "Alusru, you know what I am trying to say, so please try to be a good girl and help your mother, and I think you will like our guest. He is very nice and was in our wedding. He was my best man. He also did many things for the people during the war, but he can tell you more than I am able to say. His name is Allen, and he really likes your mom's cooking."

I had never heard his name, and I was interested to meet this Mr. Allen. The day came, and a big truck stopped at our door. A good-looking man with a beard jumped out and rang the bell on our house. Daddy went to open the door, and I could hear both men laughing. When they entered the kitchen, Mr. Allen was speechless, and he looked at Mom. He was very surprised when he saw Mom. He gave her a big hug and said, "Oh, Anna Margareta, you look great! You look just like a beauty queen. Look at you! Remember, my offer is still good—if this guy is not good to you all the time, give me a call. I will come and take you in my arms and treat you better than anyone else."

Mom laughed, but I had no idea why this Mr. Allen wanted to take Mom away from Daddy. I looked at the strange guest and decided to watch him to find out why he came to visit us. But I knew I needed to be nice.

When Mr. Allen saw me, he was speechless again, and his mouth was wide open. He starred at me.

I forgot all my promises to be very nice to the guest, and I said, "Why are you looking at me, and why do you want to take my mom away from Daddy? She is my mom and Jorg's mom and George's mom, and Daddy is her husband and our daddy, and Mom and Dad love us. I think you should go home to your kids."

I will never forget Mr. Allen's face and the loud laugh. Mom gave me a big hug, and Dad said, "You better apologize to Allen, Alusru. You can't be rude to our guest, and this was not very nice."

But Mr. Allen laughed again and said, "Martin, your daughter is proud of you both, and then he gave me a big hug and put his hand on my head and said, "Alusru, you don't have to be afraid that I will kidnap your mom. I've known your mom and dad for a long time, and your dad is my best friend. Friends don't hurt each other; they will be good and watch out for each other. So if I take your mom away from your dad, I would not be a good friend to your dad. I love your mom because she is also my friend. I was only kidding and your mom knows it. I think it is okay that you told me to stay away from your mom, and I hope you will tell that to every guy because your mom is a wonderful lady in and out. She deserves that compliment.

"And by the way, I knew your mom when she was a very little girl with her hair in two braids. She always had different bows in her hair. Your mom and I went together to kindergarten. And to answer your question, I don't have children because I had no time to start a family because I was living in the woods and was hiding from the people."

I looked at Mr. Allen and said, "Why were you hiding? Did you do something wrong?"

Daddy said, "Alusru, you are rude again. You can't ask Allen a question like that. He didn't do anything wrong. I think he is a hero because he was helping people and saving many children during the war. He was hiding them from Hitler and the Nazi regime."

Mr. Allen said, "I had a chance to leave Bochum before they could catch me. If they would have caught me I would have been tortured and shot because they were after me when the war started. Well, the good Lord protected me, and without God's help, I would have never made it. It was not easy to leave everything behind, and it was a long time, but I believed that this was my duty to save children.

"First I went to South Germany, and with a good friend of mine I found a secret tunnel to the mountain where I was hiding with the children and also many adults. The most difficult part was to keep the little kids quiet because when the SS and the Nazi troop came close to the mountain, they were listening for any noise. They found several tunnels and blew them up, and if they would hear anything from our tunnel, we would all be dead.

"Every time they came close, I prayed to God to close the tunnel with His angels and to keep all the children quiet. God answered, and when we were in danger, all the children fell asleep, and thunder and lightning stopped the soldiers from coming any closer to our tunnel. They never found us and had to return to their headquarters. I can't tell how many people I had with me, but sometimes I had thirty children and ten adults in the tunnel.

"When the danger was over, they went to the other side and reached a new safe place. Most of the time people on the other side were waiting for them to help everyone and to get them out of Germany. I remember one time, when we all were very hungry and thirsty, God gave us water and food. One of the children ran to the other side and came back with a whole handful of all kinds of berries, and we had food for everyone, and water came out of the stone wall. We had enough to satisfy our thirst."

I was looking at Mr. Allen and feeling very guilty that I was not very nice to him. I started to like him and wanted to hear more about the great time when God was with him.

Mom made coffee, and I helped her to set the table, and we all sat down. I wanted to sit beside Mr. Allen because I wanted to apologize and to ask him to tell more things about the miracles he had received from the Lord.

Dad said to let Allen speak and not to try to insist on everything right away.

"You need to wait for him to tell you more. I know it is very difficult for you to wait, but this is a time to learn patience," he said.

Mr. Allen took my hand and looked at me. He smiled and said, "I think your daddy is right. One important thing in our life is to learn to have patience and to wait. The biggest part of our life is waiting, and we will learn to have patience. You see, when we all were hiding in the tunnel, we didn't know how long it would be, and we all had to wait. Most of us prayed during this difficult time. We all asked the Lord to give us patience and teach us to learn to wait for the right moment and God's guidance so we had a chance to survive.

"But I promise you, I will tell you more about God's miracles in my life. God was always close by. Let us now have some cake."

Mom had made a delicious chocolate cake, and she knew Allen liked chocolate. Mr. Allen smiled and said, "I think I had my last chocolate cake about ten years ago, if not even fifteen. Well, I can't remember, but I still remember the taste; it was very good. Martin, you must be very lucky to have such a good cook and wife."

My dad gave Mom a kiss and said, "Yes, my friend, I am very lucky, and you heard my daughter—she told you that you can't have her."

Everyone laughed, and Mr. Allen tried to make a sad face. We all had a great time, and Dad told Mr. Allen that he was more than welcome to stay at our house for a few days, but Mr. Allen said he needed to leave soon because he had to take care of some business but would be happy to come and visit again.

I was hoping to hear more about his time in the mountain, and I tried to tell him, but Mr. Allen said, "I can't believe it— that you want me to stay—because a few minutes ago you told me to go home. Little girl, you need to make up your mind."

I felt very uneasy and turned red. Our guest made me even more uneasy when he said, "Alusru, you don't need to blush. I am just enjoying teasing you."

Jorg and George giggled, and I was ready to get mad, but when Daddy looked at me I decided to ignore everyone. I think it is sometimes the best to ignore brothers. Mr. Allen was staying for the night, and we all had a great time visiting with him, but soon Jorg and I had to say goodnight.

I remember that I was not very happy and insisted that Mr. Allen would stay, but Dad became quite angry with me, and when he got up I knew that I was in trouble if I didn't stop.

The next day Mr. Allen left, and it took many years before I saw him again. When I look back at my childhood, I have to say that I had a wonderful time. My parents tried to do whatever they could do, and my dad went to many places to get food on the table.

8

My Last Conversation with Opa

Jorg and I went to the school in Altena, and after eight years of regular school, we needed to move to another city. Opa came every three months to stay with us for a month, but just before we were ready to move, Opa became very sick and we had to take him to the hospital.

I will never forget that day, and I still can see my Opa in the hospital bed. He had a mask over his face and was all covered up because he had a very difficult time breathing. Mom said that he was very ill and we needed to be very good and ask God to help Opa and to heal him.

I was very upset, and I told God that I needed my Opa and I knew that Jesus could heal him and make him okay. I visited Opa every day, and I thought that he would soon come to our home and would live with us forever.

I remember the day when Opa told me to sit on his bed and to listen to him. In his words: "My sweet baby, my little princess, I need to talk to you, and you need to promise me not to get sad or upset because I love you, and I told you that Jesus loves you. Regardless of whatever you do, Jesus will always be with you. I need to give you a message from Jesus. He loves you, He loves Jorg, and He loves George. He loves your mom and he loves your dad. I have seen His love, and I know Jesus loves me.

"I have to leave you all very soon to be with the Lord. I promise to visit you in your dreams and to give you help and protection even when you can't see me. I will always be close to you. I will be your guardian angel, and I will watch over all of you. You see, little princess, I am very sick, and I cannot breathe without the mask and the oxygen, and I told the Lord to take me home. The Lord smiled and said, 'Soon,

Opa, but you need to talk to your little baby princess.' So, you, see I am ready, and I know you will be very sad—and maybe angry—but if you lean on Jesus, He will help you. I can see the tears in your eyes, and I can feel that you are upset, but that is okay, princess. Promise me to try to be strong and to comfort your mom and dad, and tell your brothers that Opa is with Jesus."

I don't know what it was, but I felt on the outside very much pain and anger, but on the inside when I closed my eyes, I felt an unexplainable, wonderful peace. I put my head on Opa's shoulder and told him that I love him and I will be strong, but I still will ask Jesus to help him to get better and to give me more time to be with him. That last time with my Opa was unforgettable, and every moment it was all my life like a priceless treasure to me.

When I kissed Opa and said goodbye, I didn't believe that it was forever. I can't remember when Daddy came and took me home. I can't remember when Mom came and held me in her arms, but I remember when we went to the hospital the next morning. I remember the nurse when she gave me a hug and told me that Opa went to sleep without any problems, and when she checked on him she heard him whisper, "Jesus, Your will be done. Take care of everyone. I am ready."

The nurse told us that Opa never woke up. She said, "He was very close to the Lord because falling asleep and not waking up is always a sign that God had closed the eyes of someone who really was close to His heart, and I think that your grandpa was very special."

I cried all day, and somehow I was angry with God and everyone. Jorg and George played, and I went to my room and took all the things I had treasured because Opa gave them all to me. I held the angel figures in my hand, and all the Bible verses Opa wrote on papers and in my little notebook. I pressed my little hand on everything and cried. I finally fell asleep on the floor, and I remember that I again felt peace.

When I woke up, Mom and Dad told me that we had to prepare for Opa's funeral and that we had to go to Bochum because Opa wanted to be buried beside Oma. Uncle Albert would be the pastor. Aunt Hanna was waiting for us, and we could stay at her place.

We all went to Bochum, and I never forgot the funeral service; it was held in one of the biggest churches in Bochum, and people were standing outside on the street because the church was packed. I could not believe that so many people came.

The police were lined up and saluted when they rolled the coffin in and out of the church. I was holding on to Mom, Dad, and my brothers. We all sat down, and Uncle Albert began to talk. I could see that he had a difficult time speaking without crying. I cannot remember every word, but I was surprised when he said the same words Opa had said to me so many times: "Yes, Lord, You know the best and not our will, only Your will be done. We trust You and pray to You in Your Holy and wonderful name, Jesus Christ!"

After the service, a huge group of children stepped in front of the coffin and sang "Jesus Loves Me." Every child put a rose on the coffin, and all the children called, "We love you, Opa, and we miss you so much."

Several young girls and boys walked to the coffin and put a huge wreath with red roses on it, and one girl said, "Opa, you will be missed by all of us, but we promise you that we all will try to live our life the way you have taught us. We also promise you that we will help everyone to stay out of trouble and to look to Jesus."

I was very much surprised because I had no idea that my Opa was also Opa to hundreds of children in Bochum. He helped many children to stay out of trouble and not to end up on the street.

Opa lived in a very quiet place, and when the kids needed some help, they knocked on his window and Opa gave them some help but always told them to try to live by the law. Everyone called Opa the children's guardian angel. I was surprised, and I know if we would have had TV at this time, they would have come out and told everyone about my Opa.

After the funeral service, we all went to the open grave side where they lowered the coffin covered with beautiful flowers and red roses. I promised myself to be strong, but when they put the coffin in the ground, it was too much for me, and I screamed, "Opa, I love you! Please don't leave!"

I wanted to pull his coffin back or jump on top of it. Two girls held me back, and a lady came and told me that everything would be okay. I was not so sure because Opa, my beloved Opa, was gone, and I missed him so much. How could God do that to me? Every time I asked that question I had a funny feeling, and today I think it was Opa who had given so much love to so many people old and young.

After the funeral, many people came to tell us all the great things Opa had done, and the kids told us that Opa had helped them when they had problems at home or in school. He took care of some kids when their mom was sick; he gave them money or bought food for the family.

The newspaper printed a long article about Opa, and even years later after his death, young people still remembered Opa. I still believe that Opa was sent by the Lord to become my Opa. All the things I had to face later in my life I could never have mastered if I hadn't learned all the things Opa taught me. I don't think I would be writing this book if I had not heard all the great miracles about Jesus. Opa was the one who always told me about Jesus, and not only that, he also lived his life in the same humble way. I can't tell how many times I felt the hand of Opa pulling me away from danger and guiding me in the right direction. I can't tell how often I heard Opa in my dreams and saw his smile.

Opa was only sixty-three, and I miss him every day, but I also know that one day I will see him again, and he will call me "princess" and "baby" again. I learned many things from Opa, and I treasured his little Bible and all the books he gave to me. When I feel very lonely, or when I have to face difficulties and problems, I call the Lord and I ask Him to help me. When I close my eyes, I see Opa and my prayers end in the same way: *Lord, not my will, Your will be done. Jesus Christ, I pray to you in Your holy and wonderful name.*

I never thought I would share all this with others, but I also learned that God wants us to tell people about Him, and this is also something I learned from Opa.

9

My First Love and the Day We Met Rev. Billy Graham

As I said earlier, our family moved again, and we went to another city, which was a bigger city, and we moved to the outskirts. Dad was transferred to the railroad in Outlet, and we lived in a big apartment on the second floor. George went to school and Jorg started to get a job. I went to housekeeper school because I wanted to become a kindergarten teacher. The law was that we had to learn the basics of life in a family, including budget, cooking, and raising children. We had to go to this school one year before we were able to start another education like teaching, nursing, or any other social education. I wanted to become a kindergarten teacher, and I could hardly wait to get my diploma in the housekeeper school.

During school time, we also had to work in different places—like families with handicapped children or in a kindergarten. I was very much excited, and I loved the children. Sometimes it wasn't easy, but I felt that this was my calling and that I had to learn and become a good kindergarten teacher.

But my life took a different direction, and when I was about seventeen years old, I fell in love with a wonderful boy. We went to school together, and I visited his family many times.

But it was only for a very short time because Peter was called by the Lord just before he turned eighteen. He loved to swim. I remember the day when he died. I looked up to him and called his name. I wanted him to wait for me before he jumped from the jump board, but Peter laughed and then he jumped. He hit the water and went down and under. I waited for Peter to come up, and then I jumped in the pool. Peter never came up, and several people tried to help but nobody was able. Peter had a fatal heart attack when he jumped and died before he went under the water.

I was heartbroken and could not believe that Peter was gone. When I went to his mom and dad, I was afraid to tell them what had happened, but Peter's mom gave me a big hug and told me that she knew Peter was gone. She said, "I knew that the Lord would call my son home soon and Peter was ready. Alusru, we love you very much because you love our son, and Peter loved you so much, but he also loves Jesus and followed His call."

Peter's mom's faith helped me to keep my faith in the Lord and to trust Jesus Christ. Peter's parents had a small business and Peter was their only child. When Peter died, they gave most of their possessions to needy families, closed the factory, and moved to South Germany.

Peter and I had a wonderful relationship and we always believed that we would be together forever. We wanted to wait a few years before we would get married. When Peter died, I was sure that I didn't want to get married. I was sure that I could not fall in love again because I would compare everyone to Peter, and I knew that there was only one Peter. Just before I lost all hope, I remembered the day when Peter and I had met Billy Graham in Dortmund in 1954. This man put a deep desire in my heart I was unable to ignore. He came from the United States of America. I was sure I would be meeting him again.

Shortly after I heard the powerful message from Billy Graham, I became very ill and was hospitalized for nine month. No one was sure if I would get better, and they tried many treatments. I was kept alive with blood transfusion and all kinds of medication. My kidneys stopped working and I was in a coma.

I remember walking a long way, and everything was so peaceful. I heard music and beautiful voices, and I saw a very bright light. Someone called my name, and I wanted to open a golden gate but was unable to do so. I saw Opa and I was happy. I reached out to Opa and tried again to open the golden gate. Opa looked at me and told me, "No, Alusru, you need to go back. Your time is not here, so go back to your mom."

I tried to beg because I wanted to be with Opa, but Opa said again, "Alusru, go back."

I heard my mom and dad; they were crying, and the doctor told my parents there were no more answers because nothing was helping. The coma is the last stage of kidney disease. We didn't have dialysis treatments at the time, and blood transfusions only kept the patient alive for a short time. During my stay at the hospital, I received two or three transfusions every week. I can't tell how many transfusions I received because I stopped counting. Sometimes the hospital had a difficult time locating the right blood because I had O negative and needed to receive the same blood type. I remember when the hospital gave me several times O positive because O negative was not available since it was a very rare blood type. People with other blood types could receive O negative blood; O negative could only receive O negative blood but would also be able to tolerate O positive blood. It would be bad for a woman if she was planning to have children; in most cases it would come to a miscarriage or the child would need to have a blood exchange.

Today things have changed, and a woman with O negative blood will be treated with medication when she is pregnant. When I heard my mom crying and asking the doctor how much time I had before I would die, the doctor couldn't give her an answer, and she told Mom it could be six months or a week, maybe even sooner.

I woke up, and I told the doctor that I was not going to die. The doctor was very surprised. She told my parents that sometimes a patient will wake up and be awake for a short time and then they fall back into another coma.

My mom said, "I think my daughter will be okay. I believe in miracles."

The doctor said, "I think we will try a newly released treatment. It is not very often used, but in some cases we were successful."

The next morning, I received several small injections. After five weeks, everyone could see that the treatment was working and one kidney started to work. Within seven weeks, I lost almost two hundred and sixty pounds. The medicine also had several side effects, because it was a hormone called testosterone. I had to shave my face for a short time, and my voice changed, but one kidney began to work normally, and soon, all the water retention in my body was gone.

I received other medications for my face, and I told the doctor, "My parents have two boys, and they do not need another one, because if I get more shots I will soon be turning into a boy; I rather like to be a girl."

The doctor told me not to worry because this was only for a short time, and it is a miracle that I was still alive.

When I left the hospital after nine months, most of the side effects were gone; only my voice never changed. During the stay in the hospital and after several blood transfusions, I also had hepatitis twice. This was often a problem—to become sick with hepatitis after a blood transfusion. When I was finally ready to go home, the doctor told me I needed to be on a diet for the rest of my life, with very little salt, no spicy food, or high fat. She also said that I wouldn't be able to have children because of the many medications and blood transfusions I had received.

It was okay with me because I was sure that I wouldn't get married, and so I never would have any children. I concentrated on my education and worked with many difficult children during the next several years.

In 1959, I became sick again and was diagnosed with early stage breast cancer. I had met a young man, and I fell in love with him. His name was Freddy, and he had a wonderful voice; I think that was the main reason that I loved him. When he sang, he melted my heart, and I was in another world. Freddy sang all kinds of opera songs and had no problems singing high notes or low notes; his voice was a tenor.

Since I had a job and made good money, I decided to help Freddy to get into the local conservatorium where he would have special training and his voice would become strong. Soon he would be singing in an opera or any musical.

After one year, Freddy was ready and became an opera singer at a theater in the city. I was so happy, and I thought Freddy would be the man I would marry, but I was wrong. When I was told that I had cancer, I knew that I needed surgery as soon as possible. When Freddy came, he told me not to be afraid and told the Doctor that it was okay when he needed to perform a mastectomy; he would love me regardless, and nothing would change.

Just before I turned twenty-one, I had to undergo a second mastectomy. When I woke up, I saw an old lady; she was holding my hand and crying. My mom was also very upset. I couldn't understand why, and I asked Mom, but the lady put her arms around me and said over and over, "I am so sorry, Alusru. What my son did to you was wrong, and I will pay you back all the money you gave for his training at the conservatorium. You see, he just got married, and I know that you love him. He never told you the truth."

I started to cry, and my world was falling in pieces. I had no idea that this little lady was Freddy's mother. Freddy had told me that his parents were dead. I tried to tell this to the lady; her name was Karen. She told me that Freddy was ashamed that she was his mother because she was an old, ugly woman, and he was tall and good looking.

I was very angry, and I told her that I was glad he was married and he would get what he deserved. Freddy's mom was a wonderful lady, and she visited us many times. She had a voice like an angel, but she was short and never had a chance to sing in public. I could not understand why her son walked away from his mother because she was the one who raised him, and if she hadn't had such a wonderful voice, he would not have become a star. I know today it wouldn't make any difference if a person with a great voice was tall or short—the voice was captured on records and the voice was shared with the world.

10

My First Trip to the USA

In 1960, I received a letter from my uncle who lived in the United States of America. He invited me to visit America and spend some time with him and his family. I was so happy, and I knew this was a new chapter in my life. I started to arrange things and counted the months and days to my departure. It was very difficult for me to do my daily routine and pay attention to my work. Indeed, I must say that I could hardly wait to pack my suitcase and get all the paperwork done.

My uncle had booked a ticket for a trip to New York on a big ship, and I would be protected by a travel aid person since I couldn't speak English. It was the biggest ship and was called *United States of America*.

My parents went with me on the train, and we left early in the morning to travel to Bremerhaven, where I had to board the ship. It was very exciting, and I remember waving goodbye to Mom and Dad when the ship left the harbor to enter the big sea.

During the eight-day trip, everyone had to come out on the deck for alarm training, and sometimes the ocean was very rough; even though the ship was huge, it felt like being in a nut shell tossed around the water.

It was a wonderful trip, and the food and entertainment were great. But when the ship entered the harbor in New York and I saw the Statue of Liberty, I was amazed and felt like I was falling in love with America; I wanted to live here forever.

The big vessel came close to the shoreline of New York and the Empire State Building. Huge skylines and bright lights greeted the passengers. A lady came and picked me up; she also took care of all the paperwork and my luggage.

I asked her about the Statue of Liberty and if I was able to see the Empire State Building. She said, "Oh no, I can't do that; you need to wait here for the train to bring you to Detroit, Michigan."

But I wasn't sure that I agreed to wait that long, and when I was in the waiting area I looked over to the lady in the office and saw that she was busy with some other things and wasn't looking at me, so I decided to leave (bad decision). I snuck out the door, and just in time a taxi stopped. I told them to bring me to Empire State Building. I believed that it was only a few blocks away, and I knew I would have enough time and money to make it back to the station.

The taxi driver didn't say anything, and I felt a big knot in my stomach because the longer we drove, the farther and farther we went from the Empire State Building. I started to get scared and asked Jesus to help me. He told me to get out of the car. When the driver had to stop at a stop light, I opened the door and saw a police officer on the corner of the street. He saw me, stopped the taxi, and asked me why I was afraid and what the reason was for me to get out of the taxi in the middle of the main street. He was unable to understand me and asked from what country I came. I said Germany.

The officer said, "For crying out loud, speak German."
I told him that I wanted to see the Empire State Building and the taxi went in the wrong direction. I could not understand everything, and before I could say any more, a police car came and the officer told me to get in the police car. The taxi driver was arrested, and I was afraid I would be in deep trouble. Here I came to visit my uncle and ended up in a police car. I knew I deserved to be punished, but not to go to jail.

The officer who spoke German came and told me that he would take me to the Empire State Building, and I needed to be very good and not to do this again because some taxi drivers take advantage of foreigners, drive the taxi to the pier on the other side, kill the passenger, take the money and go on with their job. If they got by, they might do it over and over again until they were caught.

I remember a few sentences he used: "You see, little girl, this is New York, and this is a beautiful but also very dangerous city. You need to watch all your things and never ever go with a stranger because this is New York. New York is not without any danger. I know you like to see the Empire State Building, and I am driving you to it to take you to the top so you can see the beauty of my wonderful city. You can see New York. By the way, the travel aid bureau is already looking for you. I called and told the lady what you did. You scared everyone, and they are not very happy because they are in charge of you. If anything would have happened to you, they would lose their license and would be in deep trouble because they did not do their job."

I felt bad, and I told the officer that I was sorry and wouldn't do this again. I thanked him for taking me to the Empire State Building. I also told him that I loved New York and that I wished it would be my city too. I said that I loved America and wished I could live there for the rest of my life.

The nice police officer smiled and said, "You are so young, and if the good Lord wants you to come to America, He will open doors for you and bring you to the United States of America—maybe even to the city of New York. I believe with all my heart with God all things are possible! I do believe that you also believe in God."

Oh I did, and I told him about the miracles God had done for me.

The officer stopped the car in front of the famous Empire State Building. I followed him, and we entered the big, beautiful hall, and then we walked to a huge elevator. It took only a few seconds to reach the highest level of the Empire State Building. I will never forget the moment when I saw the beauty of New York and the beauty of the United States of America. It felt like being in a dream land, and when the officer took me back to the travel agency, I was still amazed and speechless.

I thanked the officer for the help and for the trip to the Empire State Building, and he told me that this was a reward for him, and his kids would be happy to hear that he helped a young lady from Germany to see the highest building in New York and America.

The lady from the travel aid agency was relieved to see me, and she took me into her office and thanked the officer. I gave him a big hug and promised not to do it again. I had to wait a few hours, and finally I could enter the hall where the train was ready to leave New York and bring the passengers to all kinds of different cities and states. I needed to get to Detroit, Michigan.

It was a long ride, and I knew the time when the train would be arriving in Detroit. What I didn't know was that America had different time zones, and when my watch told me that it was time to get ready, the conductor stopped me and pointed at his watch and I saw it was one hour different. I had plenty of time to get ready. By the way, the conductor kept a very close eye on me to make sure that I was not leaving the train in any other city. I think he even checked on me when I was sleeping; maybe the lady from the travel agency had told him to watch me very closely because of what happened in New York.

Well, I was glad that it was dark a few hours and most passengers were asleep. We also got food on the train, and I bought some pop.

It was early in the morning when the train rolled into the train station of Detroit, Michigan. The nice conductor took my luggage and helped me out of the train. I heard many different announcements, and when I heard my name I knew that my uncle was ready to pick me up. I would be with him and his family for six weeks, so maybe I would learn some English and maybe I would be able to get a job in Germany to make enough money to visit America again. Maybe God would send me to this country. Maybe! Maybe! Maybe! These were my thoughts and my deep wishes because I fell in love with this great country—a country who gave honor to the Lord.

This beautiful country is one Nation under God. The whole world knew it because the proof is on all the money. America believes in God. It says on every cent, dime, nickel, quarter, and every dollar bill, *In God We Trust*! I was sure that America was God's country and God loves America. I felt very special to have the opportunity to visit this great nation.

My uncle and his two boys were waiting for me. I was very tired and glad to see my uncle George. George and Walter, my two cousins, looked at me, and Uncle George gave me a big hug and said, "So you made it, and I hope you had a safe trip. You will have a great time, and we are happy to have you here. Aunt Elizabeth can't wait to meet you, and Mary Louise is also very excited."

My uncle picked up my luggage and we all went to the car. We had to drive to Flint, Michigan, where my uncle had a very nice house with a huge swimming pool. I had never met my aunt, and when I saw her for the first time, I connected with her right away. I also felt a connection with Mary Louise; even though I had a difficult time understanding my cousin, I felt welcome.

I have to say I had a great time, and we went to many places in Michigan. I am very thankful to my uncle and aunt for the great time and for all the things they did for me. I tried to learn some English, and I heard so many times the sentence: *Shut up!* But I didn't know the meaning, and I used it in a wrong way. We were all in the pool, and Walter started to splash the water and I told him to shut up. My uncle and my aunt laughed, and from that time, my cousin called me "shut up girl." At that time, I didn't know the meaning and could not understand what was so funny. Later, when I started to learn English, I also laughed at myself when I remembered using words the wrong way. I have to say the best way to learn anything is to make mistakes. Everyone makes mistakes and no one is perfect.

I also found out during the years that most people will get very mad and defensive when they have made a mistake; they will be in denial and start to blame others. Before I had to go back to Germany, we all went on a nice long trip to Mackinaw City. I will never forget the Catholic Shrine on the Indian River with the largest Crucifix in the world. The cross was made from a California redwood tree and stands fifty-five feet high and is twenty-two feet wide. It weighed fourteen tons. The corpus was cast in bronze, was thirty-one feet high and twenty-two feet wide, and weighed four tons.

We also drove over the Mackinaw Bridge where Lake Michigan and Lake Huron come together and a big suspension bridge connects the northern part of Michigan with the main part of Michigan. The bridge is over twenty-six thousand feet long, was built in 1952, and opened up in 1957.

It was a wonderful trip. I can't remember all the things we did during my visit, but I remember that I had a great time and my uncle and aunt did everything to help me to get over my long-time sickness.

I asked my uncle why he made the decision to let me come on a ship and not on a plane. He told me that he would never travel on a plane; a ship was much better and I was his special niece. My uncle didn't know that he would become one of the reasons why I fell in love with America.

11

My Parents' Separation, Dad's Suicide

After my trip to the United States of America, I decided to become a midwife and to deliver babies since I was unable to bear any children. I loved to be a midwife and I delivered five thousand babies, but I have to say that every delivery was a miracle. I never took being a midwife as an occupation; I always said that it was a privilege and a special call to witness—to help a new baby entering this world. To see the smile and overwhelming happiness when I handed the mother her baby was always the greatest reward. Every delivery was different for me and I never took for granted that everything would be okay. I remember when I was still in the midwife school I had to deliver a baby and the mom was about four times my size. The baby was coming, and I told her to relax and to push. She pushed, I lost my balance and landed under the bed. She called for another midwife. Of course everyone laughed, and my teacher came. I was very embarrassed, but the mom said it was no problem because this happened before and it was not my fault. I still finished delivering the baby, and the mom was happy to have a girl because she had four boys.

I also remember when I was in Stuttgart working in a special hospital. After several long days and delivering one baby after another, I decided to go home and sleep a few hours. Before I left, I went to look at a very special lady. She was in the hospital for several weeks because this was her fourth pregnancy and she had lost every baby. I felt that she needed to be watched very closely, and we needed to be very alert and careful. Every time before I left, I went to see her and also listened to the baby's heartbeat. This time when I checked on her, she said to me, "Alusru, do you think that God wants me to become a mom?"

I said, "Of course, and everything is okay. Let me telephone with your little prince, and you will see nothing will go wrong."

When I listened to the heartbeat, I had a very difficult time to get a good heartbeat, and when I checked, I noticed the umbilical cord had fallen down. I had to act very fast to save the unborn child. At the same time, I needed to keep cool and keep the mom calm. The mom started to get scared, but I told her that I had the baby's heart in my hand, and the baby was doing fine. I called for assistance, and we had to bring the mom to the operating room to do a caesarean, and it needed to be done right away.

Mom was on the fourth floor, both elevators were out of order, and the operating rooms were on the first floor. I had to find a way to get the mom to the first floor without putting the unborn child in danger. I told the mom that she would soon be holding her baby in her arms, but she needed to trust the Lord and not get upset because the baby was doing fine. We needed to get it out one way or another. I was holding the umbilical cord and had my hand by the head of the baby so the head would not push against the cord.

The mom started to get some contractions, and we had to move fast. We called everyone, and I decided to call the ambulance crew to lift the mom and me on a stretcher down to the operating room. In a matter of twenty minutes, we had the mom on the first floor, and the doctor was ready to get the little prince out of danger. I gave thanks to the Lord for giving the mom a healthy baby boy. I know if I hadn't checked on her, the baby would have died, because if the umbilical cord is squeezed or oppressed, the unborn child will die in a very short time.

I still believe that the Lord was in charge from the very beginning. I also told the mom and dad if they were planning to have another child to let the midwife know that the problem with the umbilical cord could bring the same trouble, and it could result in another still birth. As I said before, I feel blessed that the Lord let me become a midwife and that my greatest reward was a happy mom and dad.

I also remember when I became angry with a very young girl. She didn't want to give birth to her baby, and she tried everything to kill her child before the delivery. When the baby was ready to be born and the head came, she started to fight me and to strangle her baby. I lost my cool and I slapped her, and I told her that she could give the baby up for adoption, but I would stop her from doing any harm to her child.

When the baby was born, I let her hold it for a few minutes and the bond was right there. The young girl became a wonderful mom, and she was happy to have a beautiful baby girl. Later, she also became a midwife, and her little girl was her flower girl when she married the girl's daddy. I could write many things about my time being a midwife.

I had also delivered twins when I was on a bus for a weekend vacation. I noticed a lady wasn't feeling well, and I asked her if she needed some help. Then I noticed she was pregnant, and she told me her water broke and the contractions were very strong. It was her third child, and they told her that she might be having twins. We were out in the country far away from a hospital, and I knew that a baby would not wait. I told the bus driver to stop the bus, and I told every passenger to get out of the bus. The bus driver was very helpful, and we both helped mom to deliver the new offspring. We had no problems, and when everyone entered the bus again, they all wanted to see the new passengers.

The bus driver said, "I am so glad that Alusru was on board, and I think I should give her a free ride next time."

I only said, "I am glad that I could help and that everything turned out well, but don't give me the glory alone, because without your help and the cooperation of everyone, we could not do it. Most of all, I think the Lord gave us all the help."

Mom was happy holding her little girls. Both babies were wrapped in several scarfs from the ladies on the bus. We didn't reach our destination; instead we drove to the next hospital to take care of mom and her babies. The doctor was surprised when he saw the newborns wrapped in all kinds of different colors and their mom smiling and happy.

I just want to say that it was scary sometimes in such situations as these, but we were trained during our time in the midwife school for unexpected situations, and in Germany the law said that no doctor could deliver a baby without a certified midwife. Every midwife had to know when a doctor needed to take over, because when complications made it impossible for a normal delivery, the midwife had to call a doctor or had to get the woman to the hospital. At the time I became a midwife, we only had a wooden or metal stethoscope to listen to the baby's heartbeat, and we had to determine if we needed to call a doctor. From the very beginning in our two-year training, we learned that having a baby was not a sickness; it was a normal process, and with good and regular check-ups, giving birth to the baby was the high point. Most moms can't remember the contraction pain and the delivery pain when they hold their newborn for the first time in their arms. I have to agree, because I gave birth to five children and also had many complications during my pregnancy and delivery time.

But I will talk about this later, and I will now stop talking about having babies and being a midwife.

After I had delivered so many babies, one day I felt a deep desire to have my own child. I knew that according to medicine and knowledge, it was impossible for me to have a healthy child because of my long sickness and all the blood transfusions I had received. But what did Opa tell me before he died? *With God all things are possible.* I decided to ask God, and I prayed to Him. I was very surprised when God gave me His answer. *Alusru, I thought you would never ask me. You need to have some patience, and don't rush anything. Just listen to your heart, and you will do the right thing.*

I had met a man in my hometown, and I liked him and thought he was the right one. In other words, I fell in love, and before I knew it, I became pregnant. I was not afraid that something would turn out wrong because I was ready to marry Harry. We had all things ready for our wedding. The invitations were sent out, and Harry's family was very much excited. His dad had a store, and he sold motorcycles and bicycles. I had a good relationship with his mom and dad. But then things changed with my fiancé because I had a miscarriage, and we never got married because he believed losing the baby was my fault. We got into a big fight, and I called off the wedding. I knew it was not meant to be and maybe I rushed things. I forgot what God had told me—to have patience and to wait.

When I complained to the Lord, He told me again to trust Him and to leave it in His hands. It took another year of waiting.

I had just delivered twins when my professor came in the office waving a newspaper. He pointed out several ads and told me to fill out the questionnaire and send it in.

I looked at the paper and said, "Not for me, professor. I can't understand anything. This is English and I don't speak English."
The professor laughed then he told me if I was interested he would fill out everything and send it out for me. He also wanted a photo to attach to the form. My professor knew about my problems, and he also wanted me to be happy and have my own family, so he thought this was a good start.

I went along with it and never really believed that it was real. All the ads came from different countries, and I was interested in the USA. There was also a photo from a young man living in the northern part of Minnesota who looked very nice. He was a farmer and had black hair—good looking. I agreed to give it a try. Deep inside I didn't believe that I ever would receive an answer.

When I left Stuttgart because I had to get home to help my mom, I still hadn't received any answer from Minnesota. But then came the first letter from Dennis, and I was surprised. It was the same picture, and he lived in a small town in Minnesota. He had a farm and was growing wheat, barley, oats, and flax. Besides, he raised cattle and sheep. I decided to answer him back and to see where it would go. Maybe this was the answer to all of my questions. Maybe Minnesota was my destiny and it was the Lord's way I needed to follow. I wanted to take it step by step, and I was going to do everything right because I felt very uneasy.

To answer Dennis's letter, I needed to find a translation office. I don't know how much money I'd spend to translate his letters and my letters. Finally, I thought it was very expensive and I started to use a German/ English Dictionary to translate his letters and to tell him things about myself.

My mom and dad were not together anymore (since 1965). I came home from work unexpectedly, and I was surprised when I entered the home of my parents. My dad was totally out of control; my mom was crying. I had never seen any fight between my parents, and I had never witnessed any bad argument, so this was devastating for me and a real shock. I loved my dad, and I was always his special daughter. He called me *Moeppken* and we had a wonderful father-daughter relationship.

I also loved my mom, and I didn't like to see her crying. But I needed to find out what happened, so I told my dad to stop hurting Mom. But Dad told me to stay out of it and to mind my own business. It was late, and I needed to do something, so I shouted at my dad and told him I would fight him because I would not stand by and do nothing. I would call the police. Dad got very mad at me, and I could see that something was indeed wrong. Dad was on medication because he had a bad cancer of his thyroid. He received radiation and chemotherapy treatments over several weeks. I tried to calm him down and to talk to him, but things got worse, so I called the police.

Mom and I had to leave and stay with her friend. Since Dad was sick, Mom worked at a laundromat where she met Edith, and they became friends. I think Edith knew about my dad's anger and gave

Mom all the support she needed, because she was also living separate from her husband.

When I talked to Mom about Dad, she would close down and not give me any answers. I know Mom loved Dad and would do anything to stay with him, but when I saw Dad physically abusing Mom, I had to help her. When things got worse, I had to protect her.

One day, I came home and dad had another woman in our home, and his sister was also there. Dad told me that he would divorce Mom and I needed to choose between him and her. I told him to think how many years Mom was with him, and I would stay with Mom. That was hard for me to say, but I also needed to help Mom.

When Dad went to court to get a divorce, the judge asked him how long he was married to Mom. She and Dad were married twenty-nine years, and the judge denied the divorce. He said, "Your wife stayed with you for over twenty-eight years and was good to you. She never looked for any other relation. Now you want to get rid of her and marry a younger woman. I think you should separate for a while, and at this time I will deny you your request for divorce."

That was the decision, and Dad was unable to get married to the other woman. Mom and Dad separated, and Dad never had a chance to get married again. I also separated from Dad, and it was so very unbelievable how he changed. He had so much hate for Mom that I was afraid he would hurt her one day. I was glad when he moved away to be with his family, and Mom could do her own things.

I tried several times to contact Dad, but every time his girlfriend denied me the ability to talk to him. Deep in my heart I missed Dad, but I was unable to reach him.

Today, I think I should have tried much harder, but I was also very angry at my dad and his family. Where did that woman get any right to stop me from talking to my dad? The last time I had a conversation with him was when I was already married and my daughter was born. Dad was not willing to try to change things and to meet with us, so I told him he could do what he wants and he would never see his grandchild. Today, I would think twice because I denied my children to meet their grandfather, and I think I had no right to do that, but I know people will do a lot of things when they are angry. Maybe I would have had a chance to turn things around, but I didn't.

Five years later, it was too late because his "girlfriend" put him in a home and tried to get power of attorney over him, and my dad committed suicide. He died in 1979. We were notified a year later. I need to say that I still feel guilty because maybe I could have helped my dad. All I can say is it was very sad to see how a long marriage can end in tragedy and deep pain. I also think that the side effects of the treatment and medication were part of my dad's problem—changing his behavior and turning love into hate.

12

1970: Second Trip to the USA, I Get Married

I worked in my hometown and had almost given up meeting someone who would love me—who didn't care that I wasn't able to wear a bikini, that it would be difficult or impossible for me to have children, and if I had a child, that I could not nurse it.

When I received the answer from Dennis, I was surprised, and I knew that he was interested to meet me. I wrote him that I needed to know what his blood type was. In April of 1970, he wrote a letter to me telling me to get ready to come meet him and his blood type was O negative.

I went to the tourist office and asked for the price of a round-trip ticket from the city of Duesseldorf, Germany to the city of Roosevelt, Minnesota. No one was able to tell me; they didn't know where Roosevelt was. The nearest place to the northern part of Minnesota was Winnipeg, but that was Canada. The other way would be Minneapolis, and a round-trip ticket would be $190. I would also need a passport.

It didn't take me very long, and soon I had all my things in order. In May of 1970, I was on my way to the United States of America. This time, I flew with the Lufthansa and reached my destination in less than eighteen hours. I flew on a direct flight to Minneapolis, Minnesota.

Our first meeting was somewhat of a comedy of errors. When we made the arrangements, we decided that Dennis would wear a pink carnation so it would be easy for me to find him. I was also wearing a pink carnation. Bad decision! Everyone must have gotten the same idea because it was a sea of pink carnations! I looked for someone with black hair, like his picture. When I finally saw him, he didn't have as much hair as I had thought, and he had a black beard! He called me his *uschi*, which means sweetheart. I know we liked each other right away. We continued our courtship.

Dennis had a farm and he worked at a window factory, which was about twenty miles from our home. Sometimes it was very difficult for me to communicate with him. He had very little knowledge about Germany and was surprised when I told him that we had refrigerators, washing machines, and dryers there. He also thought we were sleeping on straw mattresses. Maybe he thought Germany was *Little House on the Prairie*.

I was waiting for him to ask an important question, but Dennis was afraid to talk to me about marriage, and so I finally made the first step and asked him in broken English, "Why do you not talk of marriage?"

He said, "I thought you'd never ask!"

Well, he was so shy. I was surprised because in Germany the man asks first, but maybe here in America things are different, so I didn't question him when he made the arrangements to get married. I also didn't question him when we got married by the justice of the peace. I was not happy when I found out that we could not get married in the church after we were married by the justice of the peace.

I went to the pastor of the church and told him that I would like to get married in the church, and it would be great if we could get married in July because I needed to get back to Germany to get an immigration visa. At first the pastor told me that he was not able to marry us again since we were already married, but when I told him that I needed to have a church wedding because I do not believe that a marriage on paper was a marriage before the Lord, the pastor finally said that he would need the permission from the bishop in Minneapolis to go forth with the church ceremony.

I know if I wasn't so persistent we would have never had a real wedding. I wanted a real wedding dress and real flowers. I tried to find a store who would sell wedding dresses, but this was Roosevelt, and there was no flower shop or store selling dresses.

I decided to sew my own dress and to purchase the material. The lady could not understand what I tried to say, so I bought more material than I needed, and when I started to sew my dress, I had enough to also make curtains for the windows in the bedroom and living room. The material was very plain and light cream color, so I decided to buy pearls to sew on, but they didn't have any, so I bought silver-colored sequins, and I sewed over three thousand sequins on my dress. Besides that, I used one thousand sequins for the belt.

I contacted my sister-in-law in Germany, and I asked her to send me a veil, a crown, and long white gloves. My sister-in-law rushed every item to me, and she also sent a flower to be worn by the groom. I didn't have white shoes, so I had Dennis paint my black shoes white. When I asked for real roses, Dennis told me there were no flower shops in this area. The closest would be in Thief River Falls, so I told him to order a rose bouquet and several carnations for the bridesmaids.

The church was not very far, and several ladies helped me to decorate and prepare the old school house for the reception. I will never forget the day of our wedding. Dennis was so nervous and forgot that the school house had no water and we needed to bring water for coffee and cold drinks.

I also began to get nervous because the flowers didn't arrive on time, and it was almost noon when I finally received roses and carnations. I couldn't believe that nothing was put together, and I needed to make my own bouquet. I didn't have very much time and was already wearing my wedding dress.

The roses were full of thorns, and my fingers began to bleed, but I didn't care; I had no time to think about any problems. When I was finished, I found out that we needed to bring water, so I filled all the big containers I could find and put everything on the pickup. I needed to make sure they were secure, so I climbed up in my wedding dress and a friend drove very carefully to the church.

The people and the pastor thought I wasn't coming, and Dennis thought I had changed my mind. I think the congregation sang "Here Comes the Bride" at least three times when the bride finally arrived.

The pastor had told Dennis to push a lever on the tape recorder to record the ceremony for my family in Germany, but Dennis was so confused he pushed the wrong lever and put the recording on "pause."

When we prepared for the wedding, I chose a German song, and a very nice lady with a beautiful voice sang "So Nimm Denn Meine Hande" (in English "Oh Take My Hands Dear Father"). Today, I think even though we had one problem after another, we had a wonderful day, and I had the feeling that the Lord was right on our side and every moment was a blessed one.

I know Dennis was not very happy when I insisted on a church wedding, but I think he was just afraid that it would cost very much, and besides, he was very shy and didn't like to talk in front of people. We also had very bad luck with the person taking pictures at our wedding. Most of the pictures were very blurry, and so we didn't have any pictures to save. We had to drive to a professional photographer in Roseau. It was very funny because my husband didn't want to be seen with a woman wearing a wedding dress. Every time we passed by a car, I had to duck down like a person who shouldn't be seen because we were like fugitives.

Dennis was not prepared, so he took a side road and stopped at a drug store. When he came back, his car was surrounded by many kids dancing and singing "Here Comes the Bride." My husband was very embarrassed, and all I did was laugh, because I had no reason to be embarrassed—it was rather funny. I am very glad that I insisted on having a wedding picture of Dennis and me. Today, my children treasure the picture.

The first time, we got married before the law, and this was June 26, 1970. The second time, we got married before the Lord, and this was July 17, 1970. My husband had a second chance every year to remember our anniversary, and sometimes he even forgot both days, but most of the time he brought me a little surprise.

13

Pamela Born in Germany

I needed to return to Germany. I had to apply for a new visa and had to make all kinds of arrangements to move to the United States of America and also to eventually become an American Citizen. When I was ready to fly back, I found out that I was pregnant and developed many problems because I had difficulties with my kidney. Dennis was very concerned, and when I finally arrived in Germany, I went to see my doctor and ended up in the hospital where I had studied and graduated to become a midwife. My doctor wanted to do a caesarean operation right away because he thought it would be the best for the baby and for me. I did not agree; I wanted a normal delivery. I really should have listened to my doctor.

When he came the next morning to check, all of the sudden there was a problem, and he was unable to locate the baby's heartbeat. It was too late for a caesarean; the baby was in danger, and he used a high forceps and cut the umbilical cord before the baby was born. My baby had a very long umbilical cord and was almost strangled because it was wrapped around her arms and neck. This was the reason for all the problems, and I was so thankful that my doctor saved her life.

I had a beautiful baby girl, and I praised the Lord and asked Him to watch over her. My girl was transferred to the intensive care unit because she had some problems and her blood type was O positive. When the doctor told me that there was a problem with her blood, I couldn't believe it because her daddy was negative and I was negative—this was impossible that my baby was positive.

The doctor looked at me and said maybe your husband is not the father. I was furious, and my doctor started to laugh and make fun of me. He said, "Alusru, don't you remember that this is always the first thought? So far the little one is doing fine and the jaundice can be treated. We will check her blood again in twenty-four hours."

I was tired and weak, and when my family came to see my little girl, I knew that everything would be fine and the Lord was in charge of every moment. After twenty-four hours they checked again, and my daughter's blood type was O negative. The reason for the change was because my blood still had O positive blood cells, so the first checkup turned out to be O positive in my baby.

After ten days, I finally could bring my little angel home, and my mom was very happy to take care of my child. We had to make plans to go back to the United States of America, and I took a job in a local hospital to make enough money to fly back to the United States and to be ready to start a new chapter in my life.

We had to decide a name for our girl, and after a few disagreements we chose "Pamela." I had to pick a name easy to say in German and English. Pamela was the sunshine in our family and especially in my life. I was unable to nurse and I never had a problem. From the very beginning, she was satisfied with anything.

My mom loved her very much, and I could see that it was very hard on her to let us go back to Roosevelt. I told her to come with me to Minnesota and meet Dennis and his family. At first my mom thought it was not the right thing to do, but after a few weeks she was ready to help me pack and also to apply for passport and visitor visa. After eight months, we were ready to fly to Minnesota, but we could not fly direct to Minneapolis. Instead, we had to stop in New York and also in Chicago. It was bad, very bad, because United Airlines lost three of my suitcases, and I lost many things I never got back. I lost all of my midwife instruments, most of my books, and my photos and important papers. I also lost a suitcase with hand crocheted and knitted items and beautiful dresses my mom had made for Pamela. We never got any items back, and the airline reimbursed me later by giving me a check for one hundred dollars.

I was glad when we were on our way to Thief River Falls because soon my husband would see for the first time his daughter. Would he be happy or would he be disappointed? Many thoughts went through my head, and I also wondered if my daughter would have a difficult time to accept all the changes. What would Dennis say when he met my mom? I looked out the window. The plane was ready to land in Thief River Falls, and the stewardess announced that we would soon be landing. I prayed to the Lord that He would be with me and let me say the right words.

The plane landed, and I picked up my baby. She smiled and my mom took the baby's bag. I looked and then I saw Dennis, my husband. He was very nervous. My mom looked at Dennis, and I was hoping that everything would be fine. Mom could not understand much English, but when Dennis looked at his daughter for the first time, he said something that would prevent a good start for a good relationship between a mother-in-law and a son-in-law. Dennis said, "Oh my gosh, she is fat!"

I could see my mom getting very upset, and I tried to change the situation by telling her that here in the United States the word "fat" means "in good health," and in other words, Dennis meant that Pamela was a beautiful, healthy baby.

But Mom wasn't happy, and my husband had made a big mistake. Why didn't he used any other word? I tried many times to explain to him that he needed to try to understand my mom. But Dennis was stubborn, and Mom had a difficult time to accept him. Besides, most of his family was more distant and I tried to do whatever I could.

Dennis's parents lived on the same property, and his mom was not very happy when Dennis and I got married. I thought I would have no problem with his mom. When we got married by the justice of the peace, Dennis took me to his parents' home and introduced me as his wife, "Uschi."

I gave his mom a hug and called her *mom*, but she was very upset and told me that she would never be my mom, and I would never be her daughter. Well, I was stunned, and from that very moment on, I kept to myself most of the time and took care of my family.

Dennis also found out that I was not very happy with the situation, and we were still newlyweds when we got in our first fight. My husband came home from work, and instead of coming home to me, he stopped at his mom's place, and about thirty minutes later, he came and asked me what was new.

I had made a big dinner, and I saw his pickup in the driveway. I waited for him, and the food was getting cold. I was not happy, and when he came, I took the car and left. He was very surprised, and I drove out. I told him to leave me alone and to get all the news from his mom. Dennis was upset and I was angry because I thought he loved me, and when you love someone and are apart for hours, you can't wait to see each other again. Besides, he knew that I was pregnant.

I drove on the old highway and didn't know where it ended. I saw a man (I thought) standing by a tree, so I slowed down and rolled my window down, ready to ask for directions. It was already getting dark, and when I reached the tree, I almost lost all control over my car. The man turned out to be a big black bear. I stepped on the gas and drove and drove, still thinking the bear would be behind me. On the next corner, I turned and drove on the main highway back to Roosevelt.

It was very dark and late when I came back. Dennis told me that he was worried and I should not do this again, because if I had an accident no one would know where I went. I told him about the bear, and he started to laugh. He said I probably didn't know what a bear looks like because he had never seen a bear in this area. Again, I started to get angry because he didn't believe me. The next day he found out that I really had seen a bear because several bears were seen on the highway and in the woods.

When I think about all the little things we argued and fought about, I think it was very wrong, but I think this is part of a marriage, and it makes a big difference how we react to all this confrontation. If we both insist to be right, a marriage will not be good; it will end up in separation or divorce. I knew that we both had a problem and that I was not able to live this way.

I told Dennis that I would be going back to Germany and that my child would be born in Germany. He would have enough time to think about it. I would come back with our child. I would go back to Germany if things didn't change. During my time in Germany, Dennis wrote one letter after another asking me to come back. I started to learn the English language, and my dictionary became like a companion to me. I was determined to do my best and to become a good wife and mom.

Now, I was faced with new problems. I was pregnant again, and besides, I had to help on the farm. I learned to drive a tractor and to cultivate and combine. I was out in the field until late. I also had to help deliver the calves and take care of the cows and horses. My mom was still here, and we extended her visa. My baby was due in September and this was July.

Dennis tried to think more about us, and we went out several times and had a great time. When I came to the United States, I was surprised all the windows had screens on the outside, and I had never heard anything about a mosquito. We don't have screens on the windows in Germany. We don't have mosquitoes. All I can say is that every mosquito in Roosevelt found me. I started to seek something to prevent those pests from landing on me. I went out in the field with long pants and long-sleeve shirts, but those buggers found a way to get my blood. I know I never will get used to mosquitoes, but today there are more sprays, lotions and other things on the market to prevent mosquitoes. I think people got sick and tired of getting bitten. Well, I always say we need to find the best of everything and not look at the bad things. So I think it's only a short time to have this pest and every year it would get better.

I learned a lot about farming, and when I think about the first time I went out in the field to cultivate, I had no idea what I was doing.

My good neighbor came and helped me. He went up on the tractor with me and showed me every step. I had driven the tractor with the cultivator over the field for eight hours, and nothing was accomplished because I never had the cultivator in the ground. Well, I learned, and after several mistakes, I was doing a fairly good job, but it was a hard work—not a job for a woman who was also pregnant.

I know it was not good, but the work needed to be done, so I ignored my knowledge of being pregnant in the last trimester and went out in the field because I had no other choice. I had no problems, and the baby wasn't due before September. This was August, and the weather was good. I had to finish combining the wheat field. Not a good decision!

It was August 5 when I had to go to the hospital because my water broke and my baby didn't want to wait. Our first son was born the following day, August 6, 1972, in the afternoon. We called him Michael. He was premature, and the doctor was not willing to put my child in the incubator for twenty-four hours until he was able to drink and gain weight. He sent me home with my baby who was not able to keep anything down, and his weight was not even five pounds. He told me that I should know what to do because I was a midwife.

I have to say that we never ever would send a baby home who was born too early and under five pounds. I was unable to nurse because of breast cancer, and the formula I tried to feed was wrong, and my baby couldn't keep it down. He choked many times, and only my knowledge and training at the midwife school saved his little life. I had to find a formula similar to breast milk, and I ended up contacting places I had worked with in Germany, which was a lifesaver.

Before I tell you more about Michael, I need to share with you when the Lord saved my life and the life of my daughter after I had an accident and totaled a brand new Opel Cadet station wagon. Dennis had ordered the station wagon direct from the factory, and I really liked it because it was my favorite color (red), and it was the new 1972 model style with only a few hundred miles.

I decided to drive to Warroad to purchase groceries for one month because I knew that we would soon not have time because the field needed to be ready for the seeding. My mom was still here, and Pamela was almost a year old. I took my daughter with me. My station wagon had built-in seatbelts, and even though there was no law to put children in a baby seat, I took my daughter in the front in her baby seat and tied her down with the seatbelt. I remember that we had a great time uptown, and when I was done, my station wagon was full with groceries and all kinds of bottles and cans.

I made a quick stop at the gas station and filled the tank. When I left Farmers Union to drive home, my little girl started to cry, and she pulled on the seatbelt. I decided to keep her calm and said, "Honey, Mommy will put the seatbelt on," and I reached out for my seatbelt and put it over my shoulder.

As soon as I snapped it in the holder, my girl stopped crying. I turned the vehicle and went over the railroad tracks. I think I drove about three miles when I saw a deer coming from one side out of the ditch and two other were following. I put on my brakes (bad decision), but I was unable to slow down because I lost total control and my station wagon went from one side to the other side. The three deer ran in front of the vehicle, and I tried desperately to stop.

Before I could change anything, we went down in a deep ditch and rolled four times over. I was afraid that my daughter would get hurt, so I put myself over her and cried out to the Lord to save her and to take me instead. All of the sudden, it was over and we stopped a few inches from a telephone post. I was still holding my daughter and she was okay. I had lost my glasses and was unable to see enough. I remember that I felt bad because the Opel Cadet was totaled and all the groceries were thrown in front. The windows were shattered and the frame was bent, but we were okay.

I began to cry and climbed out the window because the doors were jammed and I wanted to get away from the place to find a way back to the road. I was afraid that gasoline had run out and could cause a fire. I can't remember how long I was sitting by the road holding my girl and thanking the Lord for the great miracle He just did for my child and me. This could have been fatal, but the Lord saved us. His angels stopped the accident before it became fatal.

Later, I learned my bad mistake was to hit the brakes because the gravel was loose, and it was the same as if I had used my brakes on an icy road.

After some time, I saw a car, and the driver stopped and gave us a ride home. When he looked at the accident scene, he couldn't believe we were still alive. He didn't know me, but he knew my husband and his family, and he was glad to help.

My mom was happy we were not very badly hurt, but Dennis was very upset when he found out the brand new Opel Cadet station wagon was totaled. He gave me a very bad time. Finally, I had enough and I asked him one question: "Would you still be upset if the vehicle was okay but your daughter and I were killed?"

I was not very pleased that he didn't thank the Lord for saving his little daughter and his wife. It took quite a time for me to understand that a man has different feelings and reactions in a situation like this. Sometimes a car, truck, or any vehicle is more important to a man than a person, and a little scratch on his "special toy" can cause a big fight. Well, I am not that way because I like people, and I like to see happy smiles. Yes, it is great to have a nice car, a nice house, and all kinds of things, but these are things and can be replaced or repaired. Friends are people, and they are more important. If a friend is gone forever, we can't bring this friend back. We are so powerless when tragedy strikes. I know that this accident made a big change in our feelings and relationship. Dennis was very upset, and his whole family gave him all the support. My mom was not very happy, and she decided to go back to Germany after Michael was born.

14

Michael Born Four Weeks Early

Mom left in October and bought several boxes of Pelargon for Michael. I was very glad that my baby could keep Pelargon down, but he still had tremendous problems, and I decided to contact my doctor in Germany. I called my midwife school, and they told me to take my baby to Rochester.

My husband was not very pleased, but I was glad when I finally took him to the Mayo Clinic in Rochester. Michael was in Rochester several weeks. The doctor told me that his pancreas was not developed enough to digest any formula unless it was close to breast milk, and Pelargon saved his life because it was the closest one and also had the highest nutrients.

When I came back, Michael was a year old, and he was very hyperactive. I was eight months pregnant, and this time I went to Baudette to see the doctor. My mom was again staying with us to take care of my home and my two kids. Pamela started to walk when she was fifteen months, and she had no problems. She loved my mom, and she tried to entertain her baby brother.

My third baby was due in October, and I was very careful when combining, but I also knew that the crop needed to get out of the field before rain destroyed everything. We had lost half of our wheat, barley, oats, and flax in the beginning because we hired other people to combine, and they did all of their own crop first before they would do ours. Most of the time it was too late, and rain had damaged half of the fields. When we bought our own combine, we had a very good income. When I had to take care of the field work and my kids were still very young, I took them with me to the field and put a light colored blanket on the side and gave them plenty of toys to play with.

Every time I came by with the tractor, I stopped and checked if they were okay. The kids loved to see Mom.

I have to say it was a challenge for me. Sometimes I had the feeling that my husband was glad that I drove the tractor and took the time learning all about farming. We needed to buy other machines to do a better job, so we applied for a loan with the government. They told us that we needed to build a house and also a machine shed. We had a double-wide trailer house, and it was new, but the government would not give any loan to a farmer unless they were living in a house built on the property. We decided to build a prefabbed home and signed all the papers with the F.H.A.

Our third child was born October 26, 1973, and it was a healthy baby boy. We named him Christian. He was born in Baudette and did not wait for the doctor who had ordered a Caesarian. I was happy that everything went fine. Christian was one of my favorite names, and he was a very happy baby. Pamela wanted a sister, but she loved her brother, and she reminded me when I wanted a sister but the Lord gave me another brother.

My mom had to go back to Germany. She had promised to come back. Dennis and I went ahead to start building the new house in the beginning of 1974. We went ahead to hire a crew to build a basement and pour the cement for a foundation. The house was then delivered in sections, and it didn't take very long to fasten it to the cement wall. All the windows and appliances were already built in, and they needed to make sure that everything was working before we could move in.

After all the walls were fastened, they needed to pour more cement. Then they put on the roof. When they lifted the front part of the eave, it was out of balance and fell down. The crew had to repair part of it and then finally the house was built, but far from ready; we had to do the last part—painting, wallpapering, and finishing touches—and then the carpet layer finished the floor.

During the last month, we moved our belongings into the basement and had the trailer house up for sale. Soon we found a buyer, but he had a difficult time to move the trailer house and we thought he would give up. Then my neighbor came and helped, and soon the trailer house was gone. I believe that the Lord had helped because in less than twenty-four hours, Roosevelt got hit by severe weather, and a tornado touched down. If the trailer house was moved a day later, nothing would be left, because after the storm the whole place where the trailer house was before was a big, deep hole.

I remember looking out the window. The sky was blue on one side and black on the other side. It was very windy, and I called the kids to come in. We all went down into the basement when the storm became heavy. I had the feeling that a train was rolling over the house. It was over in ten minutes, but I never can forget the noise. After the noise stopped, I went upstairs and couldn't believe my eyes. The trees on both sides of the driveway were gone. The barn on the end of the field was gone, and one of the cows was up in the tree. The ditch was a big hole, and all over, the fields were damaged.

Rex, our German shepherd dog, was on his chain and his house was gone. I saw grass driven through trees and the whole area was chaos. Dennis was at work, and he could not believe what had happened. He called it a heavy wind, but I think it was more because I saw the black cloud like a funnel coming closer and closer, and I heard the train noise. This was more than a heavy wind. A wind was not able to cut trees like this; it looked like a power saw had been used to cut all the trees down. When I saw the deep hole by the driveway, I went on my knees and gave thanks to the Lord. If we were still living in the trailer house, we would have lost our home and could have been hurt, but God took care of us and we had to give Him thanks.

Soon I had to face another bad situation, and I had to make a very harsh decision. I know many people didn't understand it, but I had to do what would be the best for my daughter. My mom came to visit again, and we both noticed that Pamela was afraid to go outside.

I tried to ask her, but she put her head down and began to cry. I knew something was not right and I needed to find the reason. I thought she had seen some animal and was afraid, but my guess was far away from the real reason.

One day she came in the house and I knew it had happened again. I put my arm around her and told her to tell me everything, and I would go out and chase the animal away. She asked me a question, and it would hit me worse than anything else: "Mom, why is Grandpa pulling my panties down all the time?"

I was not prepared for that, and I needed to talk to my husband so he could talk to his dad. After all, he needed to protect his daughter. When I talked to my mom, she was afraid that Dennis wouldn't believe it and would rather get mad at me. My mom was right. When I tried to tell him what happened to his child, he got very upset with me and told me that his dad was old, and besides, most of the time drunk, and I shouldn't pay so much attention to the statement and questions from a four-year-old girl. He said to me that if the word gets out to the people, we could get in trouble, and it would be my fault if they took our children away from us.

I was stunned and couldn't believe what he said. Deep inside I felt pain and anger. This was not right, and I needed to take things into my own hands to protect my girl. I knew how much a child can get hurt for life in a situation like this. I looked at my husband and told him that I would take care of my daughter, even if it would come to a separation between him and me. If he was unwilling to believe his child and to protect her, I would not let anyone hurt or touch my child.

I remember the day when he tried to grab my arm to shake me and to stop my anger. I took a cup of tea and threw it at him. I went out the door and left. I drove and drove and then I stopped the car and cried out to the Lord. I asked Him to give me peace and to protect my daughter. I prayed and cried. I don't know how long I was gone, but when I finally came back, Dennis was gone, and my mom was worried that something would happen to me. I decided to make some arrangements to send my daughter to Germany with my mom. She didn't needed special papers because she was born in Germany, and it would be the best solution to protect her from any harm. My mom paid for her ticket, and since Dennis still didn't believe his daughter, I decided to take my children to visit my relatives in Florida, and Mom and Pamela could fly from Florida to the Bahamas to book a flight to Germany.

I called my aunt and uncle in Tampa, and they were happy to see us all. Niame, my sister-in-law, asked me to leave Michael with her, and so I agreed to let her take my son Michael. In March of 1975, we went to Florida to visit my uncle George and my aunt Elizabeth and family. We had a wonderful time, and my mom was very happy to see everyone.

It took me about five days driving to Tampa, Florida, and we went to Minneapolis on the freeway to several states. From Minnesota we went to Iowa, from Iowa to Missouri, and we crossed over to Illinois. After Illinois we entered Indianapolis, and then Kentucky, Tennessee, and Georgia. Finally, we were in Florida. I had very little problems driving after I hit the right freeway in St. Paul. I had a problem in Minnesota to get on the right freeway to Iowa, and I also found out it was no use to ask for directions because most people didn't know, and just to be polite, they would tell you to keep on driving and to ask again.

After driving for over an hour, I came out in St. Paul four times on the same freeway. Then I decided to give it one more try, and if I missed again, I would turn back to Roosevelt. I asked the Lord to help me, and He laughed at me and said, "I thought you never would ask Me."

Before I could say anything, I was on my way to Des Moines, Iowa. The freeway brought us right into Missouri. Before we hit Kansas City, we turned east to Springfield, Illinois and hit Indianapolis in the heart of Indiana. Now we were on our way to Louisville in Kentucky and went farther east to Lexington, Kentucky to get on Highway

75, which brought us to Knoxville, Tennessee and Chattanooga, Tennessee. We kept on driving on the same freeway south to Atlanta, Georgia, and after we left Georgia, we went south to Florida. After five days driving, we reached our destination: Tampa.

We stopped only at rest areas where I slept for a few hours, and then we went on our way. I am still very surprised at myself that I drove over two thousand miles to see my uncle and aunt in Florida, and to bring my mom with me. We had a wonderful time, and I never had a problem—only when I left Tennessee, I was pulled over by the state highway patrol but actually for no reason. I was driving behind a long line of cars, and the other side of the freeway with two lanes had no cars, so I went to pass all the cars in front of me. When I reached the end of the line and passed the car, I saw that it was a police car. I passed the police and he turned on his siren and flashing lights, and I had to pull over. I wasn't sure if I did something wrong, and when the officer asked me for my driver's license, I asked him if he needed to also see my license from Germany. He had never seen a German license and was very much interested to see my German permit. He asked me why I had so many dates on the back of my license, and I told him that we had a law in the country to mark the dates when we took the test, and it took me three times to pass. This was the reason I had three different dates on my license.

All the other cars went by and some drivers laughed at me. So I asked the officer what I did wrong that he pulled me over. He smiled and said, "You did nothing wrong; I pulled you over because you dared to pass me."

I couldn't believe it and asked him if it was against the law in Georgia to pass a state highway patrol car. He smiled and said most drivers will not pass a police car, and that was the reason why the line was so long. I said, "Well, officer, I am from Germany, and I am not afraid."

He was very nice, and soon I was on my way. I know the Lord was in charge of this trip, and He protected me all the way to Florida.

When we reached Uncle George and Aunt Elizabeth, I called Dennis and told him that we made it and that I would be back soon. I also told him that Pamela would not come back; she would fly with my mom from the Bahamas to Germany.

For a short time, I heard nothing on the phone, and I thought he hung up, but then he said, "Okay, I think it is the best decision for all, as long as you bring her back when things have settled."

It was very hard for me to leave without my sweet little girl, but her safety was much more important to me than the pain in my heart. I felt a terrible emptiness and cried out to the Lord many times; only His love and understanding brought peace and comfort to me when I was all alone.

When Mom arrived in Germany, I was on my way back to Minnesota. When I came home, my mother-in-law was very upset with my decision. I have to say almost everyone in Roosevelt gave me the cold shoulder. Only the pastor and his wife knew the real reason, and they told me they would pray for me. It was very difficult for me to be far away from my daughter, and we called twice a week. She learned to speak German and talked on the phone in German, but to Dennis she spoke in English. Both of my brothers were happy to spoil my girl, and I think it helped her to understand why Mom wasn't there.

15

Two More Boys Are Born

After seven months, I went to Germany to pick up my daughter. My father-in-law was very sick, and I had no doubt that he would never have a chance to touch my girl again. I made arrangements with my mom to buy a ticket in Germany for me. I had to take my two boys with me, and soon I was on my way to Germany. It was an unforgettable trip because we had to fly over Chicago, and due bad weather we had many delays. My son Michael was very hyperactive, and he would not sit down. He disappeared three times, and since I had both boys dressed in the same outfit, it was not very difficult to find the escaped little boy. But after the airport police brought him back two times, they showed him a pair of handcuffs and told him that they would put the cuffs on him and on me if he walks away again. I had no problem with Christian; he was a very happy boy and was always close to me.

My brother picked us up in Dusseldorf, and Pamela was happy to see us. My mom had made all kinds of outfits for her, and she had bought new dresses. She really spoiled her, and she also began buying new things for the boys.

After four weeks, we had to fly back, and my little girl was heartbroken when she found out that Oma was not flying back with us. Our trip was canceled because Christian became sick and had to stay in the hospital one week with a high fever. He was sick before and had a very high fever, and this was in December. He was only two months and we were unable to drive anyplace because all the roads were closed from the winter storm. When I talked with the hospital, the doctor told me to stay where I was and not to try to get to the hospital. I was not very pleased with his answer when he said if you want to risk your child's life and bring a dead child, go ahead. I was angry and took the matter into my own hands. I put Christian with his high fever in a lukewarm bath and did every possible treatment I had learned in the midwife school to get his fever under control. At one time, the fever went very high, and my baby would not wake up. I was scared and I begged the Lord to save my boy. The Lord answered, and after a week, the fever was gone. My child was okay. I know without the Lord my son would be gone. The Lord can do anything, and He will do miracles if we believe in His power, mercy, and grace. He will answer our cry and our prayers in His way. Sometimes His answer is not what we wanted, and it is difficult to accept His decision, but if we trust Him and give it all to Him, we will have peace and find comfort in the arms of Jesus Christ the Lord.

When Christian was in the hospital, I prayed all the time to the Lord, and He healed my boy. When we went back to Minnesota, Pamela was watching Michael very closely, and he could not run away, so my girl was a great help on our way back. But when we were in the airplane, my son started to hide under the seats, and I tried to stop him. The stewardess told me not to worry, and when Michael came back with a handful of screws and nuts, I was not happy. The nice stewardess was also not happy because my son had pulled all the ashtrays out.

When we were in Germany, we did not have many problems with Michael, but as we came closer to Minnesota, the problems started again. When we finally arrived in Thief River Falls, Dennis was at the airport to pick us up. He told me that his dad Andrew had died and somehow I felt a relief, and deep in my heart I said *thank You, Jesus*. I didn't have to worry about my girl; her grandpa was no more a threat to her. But I said nothing to my husband. I decided to say nothing to my kids, so if he also had touched the boys it was better not to bring up any memories.

I was surprised when Cora gave all of us a hug, and I decided to be very kind and nice to her. When Dennis treated her with disrespect, I stopped him and told him that he could not talk to his mother in the way he did. I invited Cora to stay with us, and she was happy to take my offer. We became much closer, and she started to enjoy the kids; they were happy to play with Grandma. But my in-laws didn't like that I started to have a good relationship with Cora, and that she also once in a while went with me shopping and bought coffee for us all on her food stamps. When she tripped over a little kid's stepstool, everyone said that Pamela had pushed her, and so her daughter came from Wisconsin and took her to her home.

Cora was not very happy, but they gave her no choice. I know that this all was a money deal, and I will never forget when they came and took her. She was staying with us for almost two years, and during this time, she enjoyed the freedom and the comfort of my home. In 1977, she moved to Wisconsin, and I would not see her before she came back to Minnesota and was admitted to the Pioneer Nursing Home. We were never informed when she had a heart problem or when she needed a pacemaker. She was also very much kept in the dark when we had another child.

In 1976, Cora was still living in my house, and I went to attend a funeral of a good friend. I had seen a doctor the day before, and I thought that I was pregnant. He checked me and told me that I was definitely not pregnant. I wasn't feeling well, and during the funeral service we all had to stand up. I was in pain, and when I tried to stand up, I felt dizzy and needed to leave. I told my sister-in-law to take me home. She saw that I was getting sick and took me home. At first I wanted to lie down, but then I had another sharp pain going through my body, so I asked her to take me to the hospital. She agreed and drove me to the hospital, which was about an hour to drive because we lived five miles from Rocky Point. When we reached Highway 11, my sister-in-law tried to talk to me, but I passed out, and she was so afraid that I was dead, she stepped on the accelerator and drove as fast as she could.

When the police followed her, she stopped in front of the hospital and told the officer that she had me in the car and that I was probably dead, but when the officer came and opened the door, he could see that I was still alive. They came and put me on a stretcher and rolled me into the emergency room. After some tests, the nurse told me that the doctor needed to do an emergency surgery right away because I was internally bleeding, and it might be a tubular pregnancy or an ovary pregnancy; only a surgery could stop the bleeding. It went very fast, and I told the doctor to do whatever he needed to do. I had a girl and two boys, and if the Lord wanted me to have more children, He would find a way.

When I woke up, the doctor told me that he almost gave up and I would not have survived, but somehow it changed and the bleeding stopped. He said, "Alusru, your life was on a very thin string."

I told him it wasn't my time and the Lord stopped the bleeding. I know a pregnancy can be fatal when it is outside the uterus or inside the ovary, but I trust the Lord, and I know He was watching over me.

After a week, I was released from the hospital, and Cora left to stay with her daughter in Wisconsin. I had the feeling that I was pregnant again, but all the tests were negative. When I went again for another test, it turned out that I was right, even though the doctor told me few days before that if I was pregnant he would be, too. Yes, I was pregnant, and I monitored my pregnancy very closely. When I had problems, I asked the doctor to transfer me to a hospital with a unit for premature babies. I just wasn't sure that this fifth pregnancy would be without any problems. I was right again and was glad that the doctor sent me by ambulance to Grand Forks. It was a bigger hospital and had everything to take care of premature babies.

In February 1977, I had another boy; he was born two months early and weighed less than three pounds. I had a Caesarian operation because I had a placenta problem previously. In a normal pregnancy, the placenta is behind the baby, and after the baby is born, the placenta comes. In my case, the placenta was before the baby, and if I were to have contractions, the placenta would come out, and in no time the baby would die. So it was good that I insisted to be transferred to a bigger hospital with neonatal care units and the newest equipment like ultrasound. The doctor was able to come up with a diagnosis in the early stage, and my baby was in good care and hands. It was another boy, and we called him Daniel. After ten weeks in an incubator, I could bring my baby home.

In May of 1977, my mom came again to help me. She had a surprise for all of us, and she decided to pay for all the expenses to go on a three-week vacation trip to the Black Hills. Dennis took time off from his work, and we bought an inflatable camper. Before we could leave, we had to rush Daniel back to Grand Fork with a double hernia, and our trip was put on hold for three weeks. Finally, in the last part of September, we were ready and went to North Dakota where Dennis visited some relatives. Then we went to South Dakota to the Black Hills. My mom, Pamela, and the boys went with me to the famous play, *The Passion*. Dennis stayed in the camper and relaxed; he was not interested in going with us. It was an unforgettable and wonderful event for all of us, and the main character who played Jesus was more than happy to visit with us. Allen came from Germany, and Christian Stuckel was the director. We met both. *The Passion* play came originally to the Black Hills from Oberammergau. Only during a special time of year could people see this wonderful event with real animals and natural scenery. This was a wonderful trip, and I wished that Dennis had also seen the play at the Amphitheatre in Spearfish.

We visited the famous Mount Rushmore and the Crazy Horse monument. We went to the underground caves and many museums. Before we went home, we visited the wax museum and drove to the Badlands. We crossed over to Wyoming and visited Devils Tower. Dennis wanted to see the Theodore Roosevelt Park and museum in Medora, North Dakota, so he drove over to Montana until he turned on Freeway 94 East.

Now we were on our way home, and I knew my mom enjoyed it very much, but I also knew without her paying for every bill we would never be able to pay for it. Besides, she bought many souvenirs and paid for every gas tank. I am so glad we went on this trip. I will always remember my mom and the time she and I had together.

I remember when she got very angry at my husband because I was out in the barn delivering a calf, and I needed some help so I went back to the house and told my mom to wake up Dennis and to tell him to get to the barn. Mom did, and when Dennis got up, he was looking all over for his cap because he would never go out without a cap. It took him almost thirty minutes, and by that time, I had control over the situation and had tied down the cow and delivered her baby calf.

I know Dennis never tried to be very nice to my mom, and when he was looking for something, he drew a picture, but it was such a bad drawing that Mom never understood what he wanted. I spoke German most of the time with my mom, and Dennis was often very upset because he thought we were talking about him behind his back, but we never did. When I said his name, I was telling my mom what he likes or dislikes. My mom did my chores most of the time. She was a great cook, housekeeper, and grandma. My kids loved and respected Oma.

I feel very bad that I took many things for granted and didn't see the conflict between Mom and Dennis right away. Maybe I could have done something. I was often rather unkind to Mom and not very nice when I took my husband's point of view more seriously. Sometimes I didn't pay any attention to my mom. Today I know that I hurt her all the time and also blamed her very often when I had a problem with my kids, the farm, and my family. I know the fact is that we can handle things and problems in our life much better when we have someone to blame for it. We close our eyes, ears, and our heart so we can't see, hear, or feel the pain this person suffers for us. My mom suffered very much, and it is now too late for me to tell her how sorry I feel.

16

Finding Answers for Hyperactivity and Dyslexia

When Mom went back to Germany, it was time for Pamela to start a new chapter in her life. She had to start school and needed to get up very early because we lived out in the country, and all the kids had to get very early up when they were living in the country or on the lake. A school bus came to pick up the students. It made no difference if it was raining, snowing, or storming; when the school bus was on its way, the kids had to be outside. Otherwise, the bus was gone and the parents had to bring the kids to school. I had brought my kids many times, because when my oldest son started school, he often missed the bus on purpose. We really didn't have any problems before my kids started school because Pamela had a beautiful voice, and every year Marvin Window celebrated the Bonus party in December. My daughter was only five years old when she sang one song after another in front of over a thousand people. She loved singing and sang many Christmas songs in German. It was such a delight to listen, and she never needed any music.

I still see my little daughter in her German Trachtenkleid standing on the stage in front of a microphone looking at all the people and turning to Mr. Marvin, telling him that she will not sing before everyone sat and was quiet. So they were ordered to sit and be quiet. Pam started to sing, and her first song was "Stille Nacht." About six or seven more songs followed, then she sang three songs in English and ended with "Silent Night." I know Dennis was very proud of his girl, and everyone told him that it was great. When she sang, she brought to some the real spirit of Christmas.

Pam sang on a regular basis in our church and at special events. My mom had bought Pam a German back pack (called *Tornister* in

German) for her school books, and she was very happy to take it to school, but the kids on the bus (not all of them), were very envious, so they tried to give my kids a very hard time. Pam suffered tremendously, and I wished she would not have had such a hard time.

When Michael started to go to school on the bus, he gave everyone a very difficult time. He didn't care when the bus driver got mad at him or when he got in a fight with other kids. He often came to school dirty and filthy, and I had to come and bring clean clothes. I think he thought it was fun to get in trouble—who cared what every teacher or bus driver had to say? Michael didn't care. The more important thing was that he had fun! He kept on climbing under the benches in the bus, jumping into the mud puddles, finding a way to break every rule and ignoring all the orders. I know he was very hyperactive, but this was more than a normal family could handle.

I prayed and asked the Lord, but I was forced to take him to the so-called special doctor who put him on heavy medication and prescribed Ritalin. Was that the answer for a child with a normal body and a bad behavior? I didn't like it and wasn't willing to dope my child up with medication to be able to control his life and make my life easier. I found out that I could help him by controlling his sugar, additives, and color in his food and drinks. Kool-Aid was the first drink I eliminated for all of my children. I also took away gum and controlled the pop. I saw a big change in my son when he was home. I decided to talk to the school (very bad decision!). The principal had already started to call the so-called authorities to take my son and put him in a home with other kids where they would administer the medication and where they could do whatever pleased them as long as they had control over the kid—and eventually over the whole family. I was not aware that the school had so much power, and when they told me that our son would go to a treatment center, I believed they were trying to help him.

I had seen Dr. Feingold on TV, and he was sure that Ritalin was not the answer and gave easy-to-follow answers and guidelines.

I ordered two books and gave one to the school. I also went once a month to Minneapolis to a special health food store to buy special candy treats and ingredients for my son's daily food. I wanted to follow Dr. Feingold's recipes exactly, and I sent all kinds of food with him to eat on a daily basis during lunchtime in the school, but the school took his lunch, tossed it, and gave Michael all kinds of artificial food, never eliminating high sugar and color. So the result was that he was running wild in the school, and to get him under control so the other kids wouldn't be bothered, the teacher tied my child on a little chair and put him in the hallway, far away from the classroom.

I came unexpectedly to the school and found Michael in the hall. I thought at first he was being punished for not doing what the teacher had told him to do, but why was he here when his class was upstairs? I could not get an answer from the teacher, so I decided to come again unexpectedly to check. Again, my son was out in the hall, and I could see that he had used his little chair where he was tied down to move from one side of the hall to the other. I went straight up to the teacher and told her to tell me why my son wasn't allowed to be with the other kids in the classroom. I didn't have to wait for her answer because one little boy laughed and said he is bad and he can't sit still, so he has to sit in the hall.

I was very upset and I asked the teacher, "If my child was not in the classroom, how do you expect him to learn? You can't control a child by taking him or her out of the society."

The teacher was not willing to talk with me, and I just had the feeling that something was not right. I felt a big black cloud over my family. I tried very hard to find any answer, and it was impossible to get help. I know it also had a lot to do with my nationality. Many people hated Germany because they had lost friends or relatives during the war in Germany; the word Nazi was not forgotten. Most thought all Germans were Nazis. Of course, they thought I was also a Nazi and needed to go back to Germany.

My children were called Nazi kids many times and suffered very much. When I started to fight back, I was all alone, and my husband was not willing to fight. He was not willing to protect his children, so I was always the one who declared war against anyone who tried to hurt my children.

When I was out in the field, I had to hire someone to watch the children when I was unable to take them with me. Christian had just started to walk, and we needed to get the combining done, so I hired a young mother to watch Chris while I went out in the field, but something went wrong and I had to drive the combine home. When I came, I saw the lady outside but I didn't see my son. When I asked her, she told me that he was in the house. I went to look, but his playpen was empty, and I felt a lump in my throat when I heard a noise in the basement. I rushed to the steps and my heart almost stopped beating. I saw my sweet little baby on the bottom of the floor in the basement. He was not moving and I feared the worst. I went down thirteen steps and fell on my knees. I held my child's hand and cried. I put my hand under his head and lifted him off the cold cement floor. He opened his eyes and started to cry. I knew he was not very badly hurt, and deep in my heart I told the Lord *thank You,* because He had caught his body before it hit the floor, and He had saved my baby boy. He stopped the combine and sent me back to be with my boy who needed me.

Dennis came home, and I told him what happened. We got in a big fight, and I made it very clear to him that we needed a door or a gate to the basement. He walked out, and I told the lady she needed to watch the children better and never leave them alone in the house. She snapped at me and called me an overly protective, stupid German, so I told her to leave. It was a bad mistake, and I found out later why.

When Chris was ready to start school, he started out in the home head-start program. He was doing very well, but when he had to read and write, he had a problem, and all his writings looked backwards or mirror writing. His numbers were also backward, and he had a very difficult time to tell the difference between distance and high and low. He had no problem climbing up, but coming down was a totally different situation for him. He also was not able to ride a bike. I tried to find some answers, and when I talked with the teacher and the principal, I was told that my son was brain damaged, or in simple school language, he was retarded. I would not accept that statement and searched for other answers.

I heard so often the word dyslexia, and I studied the symptoms and treatment. It was a balance problem in the inner ear canal, and the cause was unknown. When I looked it up in a dictionary, I could not find very much. It said, "Impairment in one's ability to read." Well I think that was not enough to call him retarded.

I saw something on TV one day. Dr. Harold Levinson from New York talked about a treatment for children with dyslexia. I decided to call him, and soon I made an appointment for Chris to see him in New York. We made the arrangements to fly to New York and to get him all the help he needed. I was amazed when the doctor diagnosed Chris right away with a classic case of dyslexia. We were all in the same room and looked at a picture. It was a street with a bridge and some cars. The doctor asked Chris to tell him what he was seeing. I looked at the picture and could not see any change, and when my son told the doctor that the bridge was walking and the cars were all upside down, I could not believe it. But the doctor stopped me from saying anything; he told me that he was expecting my son would say that because that was what he was seeing, and it made it very easy for him to get the right diagnosis. He explained to me all the facts and reasons. He told me after my son was on the medication for four to six weeks, he would be able to ride his bike and to climb up and down any tree, because it would help his inner ear balance problem. After the treatment, he would be able to read and write like anyone else.

I was very happy, and before we left the big city, I went with him to the big Empire State Building. We also tried to visit the Statue of Liberty, but it was closed for renovation, so we went on a boat close by. I know that Chris also fell in love with New York and will always remember his trip there. To this day, he still talks about the Statue of Liberty. After we came back, he was drawing all kinds of pictures, and he put the Twin Towers and the Statue of Liberty in most of his pictures.

We had a great time in New York, and I thought now with the help of Dr. Levinson, all the problems were under control. Soon Chris would enjoy riding his bike and reading a book, but this was not so, and it was just the beginning of pain, suffering, and false accusation. It was another way to show the anger and resentment against me because I was fighting back to protect my children and my family. In people's eyes I was a German Nazi, and besides, I was an unfit parent. I should listen to others and put my child on medication instead of taking sugar and Kool-Aid away, because these were good for children. I couldn't believe that people began to testify against me. When I look back at the time, I still can feel the deep pain in my heart, and only when I was by myself did I call out to the Lord. Sometimes I could feel His presence, and that gave me the strength and power to go on.

When I became pregnant again, I was very happy, and when the social office worker told me that I should not have another child because of all the problems I had with my two boys, I kicked her out of my home. I was angry and very much hurt (bad decision!). I found out later that the social worker had declared war against me because, in her eyes, I was an unfit parent, and I was not willing to put my child on Ritalin, which was ordered by the so-called child specialist!

At this time, she had much power over my family. I was from Germany, and there was no doubt in her mind that I was abusive to my children because of my nationality. I was willing to fight back, and the first strike against her order was that I gave birth to another child instead of terminating the pregnancy.

17

God Gives Us Ricky and Takes Him to Heaven

Ricky was born July 15, 1981, and he was like a wonderful sunshine in our family. Everyone loved Ricky and his sweet smile. He loved Jesus, and I know Jesus loved my boy. Ricky prayed in his way every day for his brother Michael, who was taken out of our home and put in foster care. He could not understand why he couldn't live in our home, so he prayed for him. He was very close to the Lord and touched many people with his beautiful smile. He was only three years old when I felt that he was different from other children. We had a German shepherd dog, and he had cancer. One day my husband made the decision to take care of the dog and he shot him. He decided to dig a hole and bury Rex. Ricky saw Dennis digging, and so he asked him what he was doing. Dennis told him that Rex had died and that he was digging a hole to bury Rex. Ricky was not very happy and told me, "Mommy, Daddy is putting Rex in a hole; he is only sleeping."

I decided to let Ricky know Rex was gone, and I went with my boy to see Rex. I tried to explain to him that a body needs to be buried, and Rex had died. Now Daddy had to put him in the hole, and we could put flowers on his grave. For a short time, I heard nothing from my little boy and thought this was all I needed to say, but Ricky looked in the hole, turned around, held onto me and cried, "Mommy, Mommy, when I die, don't put me in a hole."

I was surprised, and I said, "Why are you afraid? You don't have to be afraid. You are not dying, and when you are dead, you can't feel anything because it is only your body."

But Ricky began to cry, and I had to promise not to put him in a hole. He saw a little worm and told me, "Mommy, I don't want the worms eating me."

At this time, I had no idea that I needed the Lord more than ever. I never thought that this was the way the Lord started to prepare me for making the right decision a few months later.

Today, I think that God's mercy and grace gave me the strength I needed the following years, like when I had to fight the social office. They had made up their minds that I was an unfit parent and that all my boys needed to be put in foster care. My oldest son was in and out of foster care and went to thirteen different foster and group homes. My son Christian went to a camp, and I was told that I needed to let him go because he would be with his brother Michael, and he would have a wonderful time because Michael would come home with him after the camp. I thought this was a great decision to let Chris go, but it was not! It was a very bad decision! My husband was against it, but I told him that we should do it because Chris needed to be with other children, and so we let him go.

I wish I would have listened to Dennis. Maybe things would have turned out differently, but I thought the social office worker was trying to help families, and so I went along with her and gave her the green light to do what she had planned. She wanted to take all my children away from me and needed to start with Chris. He was never abused in our home, but he was very much abused in the camp and also sexually molested by other boys in the camp. They took my son and tried to interrogate him so that they would have enough evidence against me to prove that I was an unfit parent and they could remove all my children. The social office worker had it easy because her brother was the deputy sheriff in the city. Chris also did not receive his medication to help him with dyslexia, and so he had a very difficult time to read, write, and participate in other activities.

They tried to make a tape recording where my son would say anything against me. They went so far as to put words in his mouth. One of their accusations was that I had sexually molested him. Dennis and I had access to the tape recording, and we became very upset when we heard the interrogation. I know my son suffered a lot, and it was I who gave them the permission to do it to him.

After four weeks, we had everything ready to celebrate my oldest son's birthday because it was time for the boys to come home. I never ever will forget that day. Everyone was waiting for the boys, and the table was set. The presents were wrapped in colorful paper, and on the wall we had put *WELCOME HOME* and *HAPPY BIRTHDAY*. We were all waiting, and it was almost five, but no one was here. Dennis decided to take the tractor and do some field work, and I was getting very nervous and concerned.

Daniel went to the big window in the living room, and after a few minutes he told me that he could see a police car, two other cars, and another police car coming down the road. I laughed and thought he was kidding, but it was true, and our dog started to bark when the cars drove in our yard.

Before I was able to open the door, two police officers with pulled weapons entered my home, followed by the social office worker and two other officers. They told me that they must take Daniel and put him under protective care; it was an order by the court, and soon they would have another order to take the baby boy because there was enough evidence against me that I was abusing my boys.

I was very angry and tried to stop everything, but it was impossible. I was not able to say goodbye to Daniel, and Ricky started to cry. Pamela was questioned by the police, and they asked her if she had ever seen me naked running to the house.

She looked at the officer and told him, "My mom is never naked; she has always her clothes on."

Dennis came back from the field, and he was also very angry when he heard the police question his daughter. He was furious when they took Daniel. Immediately, we called a lawyer and had no other choice but to fight back for the sake and wellbeing of our children.

I could not believe this was real, and I had the feeling I was not able to take the accusation. I loved my children and I was now angry and very much hurt. Since I was writing for our local newspaper, immediately I wrote a letter to the editor and had some support from some readers. This was what I wrote:

To all who have children! I look at his toys, I look at his little shoes, I see his small footsteps in the sandbox where he played last Thursday. Now he is gone and we don't know where they took him. In my dreams I see Daniel, his frightened face white, his big blue eyes filled with tears, I hear his cry, "Mommy I didn't do anything, why do the police take me away from you, Daddy, Pam and Ricky? Why do I have to leave?" This all seems to be a bad dream, but it is true and it happened to our family on August 18, 1983 between 6:30 and 7:00 PM. Two local deputy sheriffs came to pick up our little son Daniel. We were waiting for Christian and Michael to celebrate Michael's birthday. The two boys went to a summer camp and it was time for them to return home. But instead, the social office worker filed charges against us for being guilty of child abuse, and she took Daniel. In the past, we had problems with the social office, and our son Michael has been away from home for over three years because of being hyperactive. We thought we would get some help in how to deal with a hyperactive child, but all they did was put my son on heavy doses of Ritalin and cut contact to his mom, dad, brothers, and sister. Michael is very much confused and hurt. He didn't know what more to say to us, how to call us or other family members. He had to say to too many people, "Mom" and "Dad." We tried to understand, and we thought it was a good step to unite the family when Christian went to spend time with his older brother. I can't tell how much I regret this decision, because it was a setup by the social office, because we didn't do what they ordered us to do, and I dared to refuse to terminate a pregnancy. Now we have to face the facts of being charged with this terrible crime— child abuse! The boys were all three put in foster care, and we are not allowed to contact them. In 1970, I came to this country. Dennis and I were married, and in 1971, I emigrated from Germany. I had very little knowledge about America and the language, but I had learned in Germany very much about the land of freedom, and I thought it was the same as we have in Germany; no one has the right to tell you how to dress, what to eat, and where to sleep. Now, I have the feeling that this country is more like East Germany. You only have freedom when you do what other people tell you to do. God is my witness! I have never done anything to anyone, and especially not to my children, that would have hurt or harmed them. I love all five of my children. I never could write all this if I felt in any way guilty. Who gives the social office worker the right to break families and take away innocent children from their parents? All because of spreading nasty rumors and fantasy stories. I understand that children need to be protected if they are living in danger, but I also think the parents need to be protected when being charged with false evidence. It is very hard for a family to live a happy life under such heavy stress. To lose children through tragedy or an accident is heartbreaking, but to take children out of a lovely home away from Mom, Dad, brothers, and sister on very slim evidence is terrible and cruel; it leaves scars for life on both sides. Prevent child abuse, but, please, also prevent family abuse, and help families deal with difficulties and keep families together! We need you! Think, this can happen to you also.

My letter and cry for help was published, and we received supportive cards and letters from people, and friends tried to help us. However, the social office denied us having regular contact with the boys, and we were devastated. Ricky was very close to Chris and could not understand why his brother was gone. He said all the time, "I want Tistan," because he couldn't say Christian, and it was very difficult for me to explain why the boys were all gone.

I said before that none of our children was abused in our home, but Chris was beaten by a foster parent when he cried for me. Soon, we had our first day in court, and I was sure that everything would be okay because I had never abused my children, and no one could say

I did. But boy was I wrong! The social office worker had so many people testifying against me, including the school and the pastor from the church (she was the pastor in our church and had called the social office worker to let her know that she saw me in the front row of our church masturbating my son Chris). It was a totally false accusation, but it was put down as evidence since it came from the pastor of a well-known church.

The truth was that Chris had to go to the bathroom, and he needed to wait until the pastor was done because she would not allow anyone to interrupt when she was speaking. Chris started to wiggle back and forth, and I finally picked him up and put him on my lap. I told him to sit still, and he was holding himself, so I put my hand over his hand and told him again to sit still; he needed to wait. But the judge accepted the statement from the pastor because a pastor would tell the truth, and nothing but the truth, because she was God's servant.

My sister-in-law tried to get out of the court before she was called to testify, but she was stopped and had to testify against me. She knew that it was all wrong, but she had to help the social office because the social office worker was the local sheriff's wife. She told the court that she saw me trying to choke my son Michael when he was a little baby, but she stopped me and took him away—false statement! The truth was Michael was choking all the time, and I had to do mouth to mouth resuscitation because he was blue and stopped breathing. My sister-in-law came when I had to do it, and she never saw it when my baby was blue and choking. She tried to stop me, and I got mad at her; otherwise my son could have died and I had no time to explain it to her.

Michael was born four weeks early, and he had a problem with his pancreas; he was unable to digest his formula, so he put his fist in his mouth and began to choke—almost every day—until I got help with feeding him the formula I received from Germany and later the help from the Mayo Clinic in Rochester.

Other people told the court that I had tied my son in front of my car and drove it; he fell down and I was still driving. They thought I planned to kill him. The truth was that Michael was on his tricycle, and I took my car to look for him and drove very slowly behind him, because he didn't want to get in my car. That was no reason to assume anything bad. Well, the judge did not believe the people and so he dismissed this testimony.

My daughter was with us in the court, and my little boy Ricky was sitting on my lap. He was very quiet and smiled at the judge sometimes. He kissed his hand and blew the kiss to the judge. I had to testify, and Dennis was very worried. Pamela told the court she was living in our home and she loved her family very much, but the court made the decision to leave my children in foster care until the next hearing.

It was late when we left the court, and I was on the stand for over four hours. Deep in my heart I felt very lonely, but in my mind I was ready to fight for my children and to get them back home where they belong. My husband was not a warrior, and he was afraid to fight, so I put on the armor and helmet and started to be ready for the "lion."

I asked the Lord to help me and to give me all the strength, wisdom, and also the patience I needed. I remember this day, because this was the first day when I went out in the field to cultivate, and when I felt a gentle touch and had a deep desire to pray and cry out to the Lord.

I also wrote my first poem when we had so many problems with the social office, and this was just the beginning of pain and suffering I had to go through, because I was alone and had no one to turn to. All I had done was protect my daughter from her nightmare with her grandpa.

I would like to share the words with all of you because I began to sing it (with the melody of "Amazing Grace"):

I walked with Christ in Germany
When I was still a child.
He is my Lord, and I believe
The son of God is Christ.

The Lord, He saved so oft my life.
No harm could come to me.
When I fell down the mountain cliff,
His angels were with me.

One day He came and took my hand,
He said, you follow Me.
I send you in another land.
Don't be afraid, trust Me!

I said, my Lord, I go with You
Wherever it will be,
But I will miss my family
And miss my Germany.

The scripture said, leave Mom and Dad
And trust and follow Me.
I left my friends, the Lord, He called
He called me over sea.

So many days, so many nights
I cried, Oh Lord, why me?
I was alone, I missed my home,
And far was Germany.

These were the first words I wrote September 19, 1975. Later, after Ricky died, I added more words to it and revised it in 1985. Here are the words the Lord gave to me when I was devastated:

> They took away my little boy.
> He died when he was three.
> The Lord, He touched my broken heart.
> He said, My child, trust Me.
>
> Then God said soft, My little child,
> Remember Jesus Christ?
> He came to Earth, was crucified;
> He died for you, My child!
>
> My God said loud and clear to me,
> There is no need to fear.
> I am your Lord, I love you, dear;
> Give me your pain and tear.
>
> I gave myself to Jesus Christ.
> Now He will work on me.
> Each day, each night, He calls on me
> Until eternity.
>
> The Lord may call on you one day,
> Might send you over sea.
> Remember what I said today:
> How great thou Art can be.
>
> Give heart and soul to Jesus Christ
> Who died and set you free.
> He gave His life, He shed His blood
> On the cross from Calvary.

I have to say that this poem was just the first answer when I was crying out to the Lord, and it helped me to give it all to Him. Step by step, He guided me in the right direction.

The first thing we did was move to another county so the social office worker would not be in charge, and another worker would take over. It was not easy for us to leave our home and find another, but we had to do it, and after we moved, I needed the Lord more than ever before. I had to lean on Jesus because Ricky, my little boy, became sick. After many misdiagnoses, very terrible, hurtful accusations, pain, and tears, my sweet little baby was diagnosed with leukemia.

Leukemia was the number one killer of children, and the diagnosis was not good because there was no cure for this disease. Ricky was a sweet little angel, and when I went to see the doctor in Roseau, I was told if I would stop beating my child, he would not be sick. Ricky was very upset, and he told the doctor, "My mom never panks [spanks] me. My mom loves me very much."

The doctor did not agree and pointed out bruises to me, and told me that he could see I had beaten Ricky in his face, leaving a bruise on his ear and forehead. I saw the bruises, and I tried to tell the doctor that Ricky had bumped his head on a chair, and this was the reason for his bruises. The doctor didn't believe me and never checked any other symptoms like low fever or several hernias. In his mind, there was nothing wrong with my baby. I was abusing him, and that was his final diagnosis.

I had to bring Ricky to the hospital again the same day, and my friend Jo Ann went with me. I had a different doctor, and she was very upset that no one ever ordered a blood test. She immediately admitted my child to the hospital and ordered several tests, including a spinal tap. My friend went home and I stayed with my baby. Ricky never cried, and he told the doctor, "My mom never panks [spanks] me. My mom loves me, and Jesus loves me, and I love you."

The doctor gave him a hug and told him, "You are a sweet little boy, and I know that Jesus loves you, and I know that your mommy loves you very much. I need to talk to your mommy, and, Ricky, I love you, and I will try to make you better."

I could see that she had a difficult time being strong, and I saw that she was crying. Ricky looked at her and asked her if she was a mommy. She told him that she had two little children. Ricky told her if she had to go to the bathroom she could go; he would wait and she didn't need to cry. I had to explain to her why Ricky had asked her.

The doctor gave me a hug and told Ricky, "I promise I will go to the bathroom."

When I talked with her, I was almost unable to stop crying because what I had feared became reality, and the blood tests were positive. My little baby, my sweet little angel, was diagnosed and he was very sick. He had leukemia.

The next day, we had to drive to Grand Forks, and two days later, I took a plane to Minneapolis, and my child was transferred to the University Hospital for all kinds of tests and treatments. I had to answer many questions, and when the oncologist asked me if I ever noticed that my boy had a hernia, I told him that he had a hernia seven times, and the doctor in Roseau would not believe me. The oncologist said he wished I would have brought my child when he had the first hernia.

I ask him what a hernia had to do with leukemia, and besides, he only had a hernia for a short time and then it was gone. The doctor told me that sometimes a hernia is an early sign for leukemia; it is where the cancer hides. We were staying at the Ronald McDonald House, and I had to take Ricky on a regular basis to the hospital for treatments. At first, there was hope that my child would be better, but then it went badly, and Ricky was admitted and had to stay at the hospital. Since he needed many injections, a tube was inserted in his stomach for easy access to his veins and bloodstream.

Every day, we went to the chapel, and I prayed to the Lord and asked Him to heal my baby. Ricky wanted to step on Jesus' windows because the chapel was round and the windows had beautiful colored glass; it looked like a rainbow on the floor in front of the cross. I can't remember how often we went to the chapel, but I know this was the only place where I found comfort and peace, and where my little boy was happy. I will never forget the time I spent with him at the chapel, and I will never forget his smiles and his words when he walked over all the different colors. He loved the bright yellow and red, and he told me the green was the grass in Heaven, and the blue was the angels in the clouds.

When he sat on the red and yellow, he told me that the red was roses and the yellow was Jesus, and He was sitting in the light in the roses. Ricky told me that Jesus was smiling and that He was waiting for Him.

I remember the last day when we went to the chapel and Ricky was in a wheelchair, and I had to lift him out and sit him on the yellow color. My little boy smiled and talked to Jesus. He told me that Jesus was holding Him and that he was going to be with Him, and he would never be in pain again.

I had a very good friend, and we prayed all the time, but she did not believe that Jesus was real. She only prayed with me because it felt good. Her boy was in and out of the University Hospital, and when he was very sick, I asked the Lord to give me some words to write to give to her to comfort her and read when the pain became bad. The Lord gave me this poem called "Faith."

It is so easy to love the Lord when our life is sunny and bright.
It is so easy to thank the Lord when darkness turns to light.
It is so easy to trust the Lord when love and peace fills the day.
It is so easy to walk with the Lord when He carries us all the way.
It is so easy to talk to the Lord when He answers without delay.
But what will you do when darkness comes over you?
Will you have faith and still love the Lord?
When doubts surround you night and day?
Will you trust the Lord when He doesn't answer when you pray?

Will you still talk to the Lord when your way leads to Calvary?
Will you still follow the Lord when you see your cross on the hill?
Look at the Lord. Be still, have faith!
He will give you comfort and strength.
He will surround you with peace, mercy, and grace.
Give it all to Him and have faith.

I gave this poem to my friend, Maggie, and told her that she needs to trust the Lord in every way, and that He will comfort her when she needs comfort.

My friend took the paper, gave me a hug, and told me she would try to believe that the Lord will give her more time and help her to lean on Him.

The next day, her son Steve was feeling better, and after two days all his tests showed improvement. This was just like an answer to our prayers, and I told my friend that God is in charge of our children and each child belongs to Him.

Maggie could make plans for Steve to go home for a short time, and I was very happy when Steve was in remission and without chemo. Just before Maggie went home, my little boy got more and more sick. When Maggie saw Ricky, she pulled out the poem, gave it back to me, and told me that perhaps I needed the words more than she. Perhaps this was God's way to prepare me.

In one way, I knew she was right and I needed all the faith and love to be strong so I could go the road leading through tremendous pain, agony, and tears. But I told Maggie to keep the poem because the Lord gave me the words to comfort her, and besides, she might need the words one day, or she might meet someone who also needed the Lord.

Maggie gave me a long hug and told me that she would pray for Ricky and me. When Maggie and Steve left, Ricky went with me to the chapel for the last time, and he was happy. At this time, I had no idea this was the last time I could talk to my baby and hold him in my arms.

When I took him back to his room, he gave me a hug, put his arms around me, and held onto me. I kissed him and told him that he would be okay because Jesus loved him, and he knew that I loved my sweet little boy very much. Ricky also helped me to love the Lord and to trust the Lord when He called my little boy and gave him wings to fly to Heaven.

He started to prepare me for the most painful moment in my life. I didn't know at this time that Ricky would never step on Jesus' windows in the chapel again. His lungs began to fill up with fluid, my child was put in intensive care on a respirator, and he fell into a coma. It was very difficult for me to see my baby suffering, and I felt very helpless and began to get angry with the Lord. I was sure all the time that Jesus was healing my baby and that he would soon be okay—home with me playing with his sister and brothers, riding on the tractor, and being on the boat with Daddy. But here he was connected to all the machines, unable to talk to me, and unable to hold onto me.

Week after week, the sound of the respirator was the only noise in his room and I felt very lonely and helpless. I took my baby's hand and tried to talk to him. I had a very difficult time not to cry, and I turned a tape recorder on. I had several tapes with songs for children. Ricky loved to listen to all of the songs, but one tape was very special; it was Ricky's favorite because it was his big sister Pamela who sang for and talked to him. She sang "Jesus Loves Me," "In the Garden," "There Is Power in the Blood of Jesus," and many more songs. She told Ricky that she loves him, that Jesus loves him, and that Jesus was with him all the time because she told Jesus to be with him and to take care of him.

The nurse put her arm around me and told me to be strong for my other children and let the Lord take care of my baby. He knows what is best, and He would be with Ricky all the time. I wasn't sure at this time that it was true because I couldn't see any change, and every day his lungs filled up more and more with fluid. Several times the respirator was changed to one more powerful. Nothing seemed to be helping, and my sweet little boy was in a deep, deep coma.

It was December and soon time to celebrate Christmas. Oh, how I loved Christmas! All my children had a wonderful time singing "Silent Night." Last year Ricky sang with Pamela, and he had a beautiful voice. He helped me decorate the tree and put up the nativity scene. He was so happy and reminded me of my own childhood.

Now it was different; my child was not able to talk or smile, and it was only thirteen days until Christmas. I kissed my baby and told him that I would go talk to Jesus and step on His windows. I would tell Him that He needed to make him better.

I had learned to use the syringe to pull the fluid out of Ricky's lungs, and before I went to the chapel I tried to get his lungs free to give him some relief. The new respirator was very powerful, and the pressure had pushed Ricky's eyes out. The sound reminded me of a John Deere tractor. I looked at my child and became very angry. I decided to tell the Lord that I was not sure I could trust Him anymore because He was not keeping His promise. I left the intensive care unit and ignored all the people who told me to trust the Lord. I didn't want to see the beautiful decorations for Christmas, I didn't want to hear the children in the hall singing "We Wish You a Merry Christmas," I didn't want to see the huge tree in the hospital, and I was hoping that no one was in the chapel when I talked to the Lord.

I had to walk a long way to the chapel, and when I pushed the heavy door open and stepped inside, I saw all the beautiful colors on the floor and the cross on the altar. Someone had decorated the altar with golden stars and roses, and over the cross was a huge lighted star. I felt more and more anger and resentment, and I stepped right on all the colors in the middle of the floor as hard as I could. I started to get mad, and I tried to break all the so-called "windows" of Jesus.

Then I began to tell the Lord, "You are the biggest, bad liar; I can't trust You anymore and I can't believe Your word in the Bible. You know that Ricky loves You so much, and You can heal him and make him better, but instead You let my child suffer every day more and more."

I walked up to the altar, pointed at the Bible, and under tears I said, "I read it in this book, Lord, in Matthew 7, verse 7. You said, 'Ask and it shall be given you; seek and ye shall find!' I have asked You, Lord, over and over, to heal my baby. I can't believe You, and I feel only anger and hate. Why did You say it? Why did You lie to the world? What have I done that You punish me? I love my baby, and my baby loves me. I hate You, and I will take my life if you take my boy."

I fell down on my knees and cried. It was very quiet, and when I looked at the cross I heard a voice and saw a beautiful light. In the light I saw two bloody hands pierced by nails and the voice said, "My child, what have I done? I died for you, and if you take your life, think about your other children; they need you. I don't punish you; I love you, and I only call your baby home. Have you ever asked Ricky what he wants?"

I became angrier, and I told the Lord that He should have told me that before Ricky was put on the respirator. Now it was too late for me to ask him because he was unable to smile, talk, or move. He was unconscious, and it was impossible for him to answer me. But the Lord said very clearly, "My child, go and ask your baby."

I don't know how long I cried, but somehow I felt His presence, and peace came over me. I went back to the intensive care unit and I was sure that the Lord was holding me when I entered Ricky's room. I took my little boy's hand and kissed it, and I said, "Ricky, Mommy loves you very much, and you love Mommy and Daddy, and Pamela, Michael, Christian, and Daniel. I know you love Jesus, and if you'd like to come home and be with Mommy and Daddy and your sister and brothers, you have to ask Jesus. He is the only one who can bring you home. But, honey, you need to let me know what you want; move your finger or do something so I know your answer."

The nurse entered the room to change his IV solution. I was waiting for Ricky to do something, but he did not move. I kissed his hand again, took a deep breath, and said, "I know, my sweet little angel, you love Jesus, and He loves you more than anyone can love you. If you want to stay with Jesus—He is right now holding you in His arms—it is okay. Mommy will let you go, and I promise you I will not cry. I will tell Daddy that you want to be with Jesus. But, sweetheart, I need you to tell me; move your finger or squeeze my hand—do something so I know you can understand me."

The nurse almost dropped the bag when she looked over at Ricky. It was unbelievable. Ricky lifted his little hand and put it on my hand and tried to squeeze it. I will never forget that moment when my child gave me his answer and told me that he wanted to be with Jesus. Here was the Lord's answer. How could I doubt His words? He told me to ask Ricky, and my baby answered me.

I put my arms around him, kissed him, and whispered under tears, "Goodbye. It is okay, my little angel. Mommy let you go. Take your wings and fly to Heaven. One of these days I will see you again. I will always love you. I will tell Daddy and everyone that you are with Jesus."

The nurse began to cry and gave me a big hug. I had to be by myself for a few minutes, and I kissed my baby and told him that I would be back. I went to the family room and I had to talk to the Lord. I closed my eyes and began to pray. I told the Lord that I needed Him, that He was my only comfort, and I needed Him to forgive me. I knew that my baby was resting in the arms of the Lord. I prayed and fell on my knees. Words came out of my mouth I didn't understand, and I wanted to stop but was unable to do so. I didn't hear two people who had entered the family room. I prayed and talked to the Lord in tongues. I had no idea what I was saying.

When I finally stopped and opened my eyes, I saw a young man holding a woman who was crying. When I stopped praying, the young man came up to me and said over and over, "Thank you, lady, thank you! You must be an angel sent from God."

I didn't know what to say, and I was very puzzled. I had no idea what the man was talking about. I had never seen or talked to them, so I said, "I am sorry if I said something, but, you see, my little baby is going to be with the Lord, and I was praying."

But the man took my hand and told me that I had given him and his wife a great message from God that their son Joshua will be healed and everything will be good. I had no idea who these people were, and I also didn't know their son.

The young man smiled and told me that I spoke very clearly, and he understood every word because I spoke in Old Hebrew—the language his grandmother spoke. I told the man that I had never learned Old Hebrew and could not speak it, so I think he made a mistake. But soon I found out this was God's way to teach his children not to judge, because God knew that I did not believe in speaking in tongues, so God used my words and my prayers to give that young couple a wonderful message. It was true: the little boy Joshua was healed and didn't needed another liver transplant. All his tests were perfect, and the doctor called it a miracle.

The young woman gave me a hug and whispered tearfully, "Thank you, lady, and may God be with you."

I was unable to say anything, so I tried to smile when they left with the doctor. Soon I was alone again, and I thanked the Lord for everything and asked Him to give me all the strength and love I needed to comfort my husband and children. I knew they were on their way to Minneapolis and might not have a chance to talk to Ricky anymore.

What could I say? My thoughts went to my family, and I felt very much alone. I needed to be strong, and the only way I could be was to lean on Jesus. He was all I had, and I know He was all I needed.

"Code blue, code blue!" I heard and I knew it was for the staff of the intensive care unit. I went to Ricky's room and saw that the alarm came from my baby. His little heart had stopped beating, and all the staff was ready to restart his heart again. I can't tell you what gave me the strength and courage to stop the process, but I did. I told the doctor that I didn't want to see my child in any more pain and nobody had the right to take him away from the Lord. Ricky was resting in the arms of Jesus, so I asked them to please let my child rest and not to try to wake him up or I would fight and stop them.

The doctor looked at me and told me it was a law to restart any heart and to try to keep a patient alive as long as possible. He looked at the time and said for the record, Ricky passed away December 11, 1984, at 14:39. Then he told everyone this was final. The nurse came and told me that she would take care of Ricky to be ready and transferred to the morgue, but I needed more time with my baby, and I told her that I would take care of my child—that I would wash him, dress him, and disconnect all his tubes and wires.

The nurse helped me, and after Ricky was dressed in a light blue gown, she told me to sit in the rocking chair and gave me my little baby. She told me that I needed this time because I needed to hold him in my arms. I held my child close to my heart, sang to him, and told him over and over again how much I loved him. I don't know how long I was rocking in the chair and singing to him, but when the nurse came back, I helped her put Ricky in a new, clean bed and a room without the respirator or all the other machines.

After a few hours, my husband and daughter arrived, and I needed to be strong for each one. We had to take care of all the paperwork and say goodbye to our baby for the last time. I can't remember how many people came to say goodbye to Ricky, and to me. Some were crying, and many doctors and nurses told me that Ricky would always be remembered as a little angel who never cried or complained. Ricky was a happy child who loved Jesus, and he told everyone not to hurt him because Jesus loves him.

One special doctor gave me a hug and told me, "I know you will miss your little boy, but he is now without any pain, and you are a very good and strong mom. I know you also love Jesus, and He will be with you and comfort you for the rest of your life."

18

Ricky Appears in My Dream, Mom Calls Me "Jesus"

We left the University Hospital in Minneapolis. I was there for over three months. My daughter was very upset and hurt, and my husband and I needed to be strong. Dennis had to drive, and I became very tired. I was exhausted and soon fell asleep. I was unable to keep my eyes open, and for the first time during the last four months, I was able to not worry anymore about my baby. I think the Lord was carrying me to a long path, and I saw a wonderful, bright light and a golden gate. It was so peaceful, and when I tried to open the gate, I heard a voice. *Mommy, Mommy, I love you.* I looked up and there was my sweet little boy, walking over roses, holding a beautiful, red and golden heart in his hand. In the back, I saw a man in a white robe with a golden crown surrounded by angels. Again I heard my baby: *Mommy, Mommy, I love you!*

I tried to open the gate again and started to cry because I was unable to turn the key. Ricky smiled and said, "Mommy, you can't open the gate because I am with Jesus, and it is okay if you cry. You see, I catch all your tears and put them in this heart. And your tears change to beautiful silver, gold, and white pearls."

Ricky opened the heart, and I saw it was filled with gorgeous pearls. Ricky turned around and said again, "Mommy, I love you, and I know you love me and let me go to be with Jesus."

I tried again to turn the key; I wanted to be with my child and hold onto my baby. Why couldn't I turn the key? I started to cry. I heard someone calling my name, "Alusru, Alusru, do you want me to stop and we can try to get something to eat?"

It was my husband. He put his arm around me and tried to hold me, but I wanted to be with my child, so I asked him, "Why did you wake me up? I was with my baby, and it was so peaceful. I want to be with Ricky. I don't want to eat. I want to go back to my little child. I don't want to live without my baby. Why did you wake me up?"

My daughter started to cry, and I felt very guilty to let her suffer even more by seeing me crying and saying all those words. Dennis said, "I understand that you are angry, but don't you think that I am angry too? I am hurt just as much as you because our son is dead, and we have to live with it for the rest of our lives. You need to think about our family and our other children. They are also hurting very much, and we have to be strong."

Dennis was right, and I had to try to do more for my family. The first thing I had to do was get my boys back. I was with my thoughts far away. My husband asked me if we should cremate Ricky's body because if we moved we could take the ashes with us. I was ready to tell him *absolutely not* when I heard a dog barking. Right after, I remembered Ricky. He was crying, *Mommy, when I die don't put me in a hole I don't want to be eaten up by worms.* I said, "If you think we should cremate his body, it is okay with me because this is what our child would want. Do you remember Rex?"

I think Dennis didn't know what I was talking about, and I could see that he was also exhausted. He was very surprised when I told him it was okay with me to cremate the body. My husband didn't say anything more, and the decision was final.

After we drove over six hours, we reached our home in Warroad, and the next day we had to make arrangements for the funeral. It was very difficult, and we had many friends who went and talked to the social office to get the boys home for Ricky's funeral. I wrote an article about leukemia and had it published in all the newspapers in our area. I also started to put cans out with a picture from Ricky to collect money for the research program in Minneapolis. It was for Professor Marriane. Leukemia was still the number one killer in children, and many little ones died before the age of four.

I needed to stay active and to concentrate on other things because we had another courthouse hearing soon where the judge had to make a final decision about my boys. He let them come home for the funeral, and Chris was afraid to cry or to give me a hug. I could see that he was not the same and was definitely abused by someone, so it became very important to me to get my children home as soon as possible. I was prepared to fight with all my power as a parent, but I was not prepared for the change in the court.

When we entered the courthouse, the judge came from his chamber, and he walked up to me and talked with me. I told him that my little boy had died and all I wanted was to have my boys back and try to help my family heal. The judge told me that he had read the article in the newspaper and I should not worry anymore. He would return my children. Dennis couldn't believe it when I told him what the judge had said.

The social office had made a request to give my son Daniel to another family to be adopted, and they had the people in court. The judge became very angry, and he ruled that the children would be returned to our family and we would receive all the help we might need to make the transition easy for the children and the parents. He also said that he would never forget the little boy Ricky with his smiles and big blue eyes, tossing kisses to him.

After the courthouse hearing and the final decision, we went home and soon it would be Christmas. All of my children would be home for the holidays, except my little baby, who was celebrating Christmas with Jesus. Finally we could start to connect the family chain, help the boys to live a normal life, and wipe out all the bad memories. However, we soon found out that it wasn't easy, and it took more than love and understanding to bring the kids back. Chris was very afraid of any boy or man, and it took me a long time to be a mom to him. He would hide when we raised our voices, and my husband was unable to deal with him; all his love went to Daniel, who was always smiling and reminded him of Ricky. Daniel learned all the things a boy needed to learn and was not afraid of anything. Besides, he was now the baby in our family, and Chris started to develop many learning problems. We enrolled all the children in a Christian school, and things were a little better.

When Michael came home, we were unable to deal with him because he had a tremendous hate for our family. He told us all the time that he hated us because he knew that we didn't love him. When I tried to talk to him or get closer to him, he told me to stay away. Over and over he said *I hate you* and *I wish you were dead*. I could see that Michael was very much brain washed, and I also had the feeling that I had to let him go back to the group home, because when he threatened me with a knife, I had to lock the door to be safe with my daughter, and I knew I was unable to change the situation or handle his resentment towards me.

Michael went back, and we visited him on a regular schedule. I prayed to the Lord and asked Him to tell me what I could do to change the hate in my child to love, and the Lord told me to trust Him. I don't know how long it took for my son, but the Lord was in charge, and He brought a person into Michael's life who had a very good talk with him and told him that no one could take the place of a mother and he should be thankful that he had a mom who cared about his life and who loved him more than anything because she gave birth to him and took care of him. I think she helped my son, and today Michael and I have a great mother-son relationship. But it took many years and many prayers for all of us before our family was united again.

In November 1990, my daughter Pamela made the decision to join the army, and in 1991, she married a soldier. When she came home, she had a lovely church wedding. My first grandchild was born in September 1992, and I was with my daughter when she gave birth to a sweet little baby girl. Pamela left the army.

My son Michael also joined the army, only a bad accident prevented him from shipping overseas to fight for his country. In September of 1994, I decided to visit my family in Germany and to spend some time with my mom who was in a nursing home. I wanted to tell her that I was sorry for my behavior when she came to be with us, but I was unable to explain anything to her because she had Alzheimer's disease and got very angry when I called her *Mom*. I tried to tell her that I was her daughter and came to celebrate her eightieth birthday. She told me that she only has one daughter and she was in America. Very sternly, she said, "So don't call me *Mom*; I am not your mother."

It was very difficult for me to accept this, but I didn't want to stay away from Mom, so I visited her every day and took care of all her needs. She allowed me to give her a hug, fix her hair, and help her dress, but I had to call her Margret. Sometimes she told me that I needed to meet her daughter because she was really very nice and she wished she could be here with her. She pointed out all the pillows, blankets, and other knitted, crocheted, and embroidered items in her room, and told me they were all from her daughter in America. Mom said, "She made it all for me, but I still wish she would be here."

I saw my mom crying, so I gave her a big hug. She looked up at me and saw the pin I was wearing, which I had bought with Ricky at the University Hospital when Ricky was sick. He wanted me to buy it and wear it all the time. It was a beautiful Jesus pin, and I never went anyplace without wearing it on my wardrobe. Mom looked at the pin, smiled, and told me, "I know you, and I know who you are."

I thought she would finally recognized me, and I said, "You do, Mom?"

She smiled again and said, "Your name is Jesus." Mom never changed her mind and called me Jesus for the rest of my time with her!

When I said goodbye to Mom, I knew it was for the last time, and she was holding onto me and told me over and over again to try to contact her daughter in America and tell her that she would always love her. I kissed my wonderful mom and promised to see her daughter Alusru soon.

I don't know how long I cried, but I prayed to the Lord to be with my mom and to take care of her. A year later, my mom died, and she never talked to anyone about me again, but deep in my heart I know that Mom is with the Lord because she loved Jesus.

When I came back from Germany, I started to work at a motel. I had no idea about any work on the front desk, and I had to learn everything. After my mom passed away in 1995, my daughter Pamela gave birth to another sweet little baby girl, and I was very proud and happy with two wonderful grandchildren. Katie was the first girl, and Jessie was born in Panama. Pamela went to visit her husband, and later when she came back, I knew something was wrong. I was not surprised when she left her husband and was ready to bring up her children by herself.

Dennis became very sick and was diagnosed with prostate cancer. He didn't want to stay in the hospital or any treatment center. I took him home and gave him all the care and love he needed. A year later, in 1996, he passed away, and I had to take care of everything without a man by my side. I know that he had lost all his desire to fight the cancer and to have treatment, because when Ricky died, Dennis changed and life became very difficult.

By this time, my children started their own lives and I needed to work more, so I became a home dialysis aid. I took care of several patients who had to have dialysis treatment twice a week. It was not easy, and it was very difficult for me when the patient died, but I think the Lord wanted me to meet all these people because when I gave them the treatments and had to take care of them, I shared with all of them my deep trust in the Lord.

One lady named Alice wanted nothing to do with it, but when she was on dialysis, I talked to her about Ricky. When my daughter was home, I brought her with me and she sang to Alice. Alice loved to sing. She also had a very beautiful voice, and step by step, she started to get closer to the Lord. She was happy I told my pastor to visit her, and he brought her a beautiful plant in a basket; it was an African violet—her favorite flower. Alice was very special, and I am glad that I could guide her in the right direction to reach out to the Lord and hold onto His hand when her time came to leave this place and to be with Him.

After I worked in several different jobs, I took another job in another motel on the front desk, and I had no problems. Pamela gave birth to a baby boy in 1999. She gave him the name Emanuel, and I loved the little prince. Nothing could hold my daughter's marriage together though, and until 2003, she had to take care of three children and worked to have enough to live. In August of 2003, Pamela married Troy, and her life turned around because he loved her three children and fell in love with my daughter. He started to take care of every need.

I tried to help Pam as much as I could, but in 2000, I became very sick, was rushed to the hospital, and transferred to another hospital in Grand Forks. I was diagnosed with pancreatic cancer, and the doctor gave me and my family no hope to get better. I went to Minneapolis to get a second opinion, and the answer was the same: cancer of the pancreas. I needed surgery and was admitted to the hospital in Grand Forks. I still remember the day when the doctor asked me if he could do anything for me before the surgery, because there was a good possibility I would not survive and would not wake up. I told him that I was ready, and if I didn't wake up, it was no problem because I would be with my mom, my grandpa, my husband, and my sweet little boy Ricky. I told him if he said a prayer and asked the Lord to guide him, that would be all I could ask for.

The doctor told me his whole staff would pray. I was ready to meet Jesus and fell asleep. I remember the music, the peace, and the smell of roses, and I remember the bright golden light at the end of a long, dark tunnel. I walked down it holding onto someone, and I heard my name. Someone called my name, and I saw Dennis and Ricky. I also saw Grandpa, Mom, and Peter. I began to go faster, but a big golden gate came down, and a voice told me to stop: "Alusru, we will be waiting for you when your time is here. God has more work for you to do."

I woke up, and the doctor was standing by my bed and told me that this was a miracle because the cancer was gone—only a pea size needed to be removed. I smiled and told the doctor, "You should have prayed a little longer and the pea would have been gone."

I left the hospital and went back to work. I have to say that work always helped me to go on with my life and to try to do my best. The Lord guided me when I called out to Him, and He gave me many friends to help me when I was tired and exhausted. But the most important part in my life was always Jesus, and I never forgot to put His name on my uniform when I worked. If I forgot my name tag, I was not concerned, but if I didn't have my Jesus pin, I returned to my home and picked it up.

When the motel changed owners, I was told not to wear my Jesus pin, and I told the new owner that he would need to look for another person because I would not work for the motel if I had to take the name of the Lord off. When he said I would offend some people, I told him if the Lord's name offended someone then they needed Him! I worked for the motel many more years, and no one was upset that I had the Lord's name on my uniform.

In 2004, I became very sick again, and it was so bad that I begged my son Daniel, who came to see me, to let me die. I was very badly treated by the nurse in the hospital, and I think if Daniel would have come a few days later, I probably would have died. He called for the ambulance and they rushed me to Grand Forks. I was diagnosed with spinal meningitis, and it was very painful. I was in the hospital two weeks, and I was very sick, but I also trusted the Lord. I knew all the time He was in charge of my life, and He would never give me a load to carry if it was too heavy for me.

19

Meeting Pastor Benny Hinn

In December of 2004, I became Grandma again. It was another boy, and we called him Jacob. I love all my grandchildren, and I am very thankful for each and every one. I have a great relationship with all of my children, and I will never make a difference between them. My daughter will always be special, and I love her very much. She was the only girl, and she was the first child. Pamela was born in Germany, and I was glad I went to Germany when I was pregnant since I developed some problems. I was afraid that things would be very difficult, and since she was my first full-term pregnancy, I decided to go to my midwife school for the delivery. Today, I think God was telling me to do it because He knew that I would insist on giving birth to my baby in a natural way.

My doctor from the school detected a problem just in time and had to deliver her by high forceps. She had the umbilical cord wrapped around her arms, legs, and neck. This was the reason it took so long, and my doctor had to cut the cord before she was born. She was in an incubator for twenty-four hours. I am still very thankful to the doctor, and I thank the Lord that He was guiding my doctor.

Pamela was a very easy-going baby, and since I was unable to nurse her, she received Pelargon and was a very healthy baby. My mom took care of my baby when I was working at the hospital until we left Germany. I had my daughter on Gerber food because that was the food we used, and I always was communicating with Gerber in Germany when I worked in the hospital. We gave samples of baby food to every mom before she left the hospital.

I knew the stores had Gerber and Heinz baby food here in the United States, and I thought it would be very easy to feed my baby, but

I was in for a surprise; my daughter would not eat the food, and when I tasted it, I could not believe that it was Gerber baby food for eight months old and up. I looked on the label and couldn't believe my eyes: "Salt and sugar are added for better flavor." I contacted Gerber and told them my concern. It was against the law in Germany to add salt, sugar, additives, or food color to any food for babies or children. Gerber agreed with me and told me that the American women would not purchase any food unless it tasted sweet or salty. I was very surprised because I had learned in my training that salt is dangerous for babies and can raise blood pressure and cause early heart problems.

Sugar was also not good and could cause early decay of the teeth. My question was, who is eating the food—Mom or the baby? Babies don't know the difference in the taste! Their taste buds and nerves aren't developed when they are newborns. I made my own food, and it took many years for this country to take salt and sugar out of baby food. Today, all baby foods are without salt and sugar, but we still fight the food industry to take food colors and dangerous preservatives out of our food and to control sugar and salt. I think it is about time to do so because who needs RED 40 in candies and chocolate? Natural colors are just fine and tasty.

As I said, I was very happy when the Lord blessed me with my first baby and when He gave me more children. I was happy and very thankful for every child the Lord gave me. I love my children the same way, regardless of their lifestyle or achievements. I made a promise to the Lord when I was still in Germany when the doctor told me that I would never be able to have a child. The Lord said, "Not so, My child. I will bless you with children, and all you have to do is bring each one up in My name!"

I did, and I still tell everyone, without the Lord by my side, I wouldn't be here today. My son Daniel has been married since 2008, and he has a wonderful wife. I love my daughter-in-law, and I always call her my special daughter because I feel she is like a daughter to me; I am blessed to have her. Daniel and Trista have three girls, so I am blessed with three more grandchildren. Each one of my grandchildren has a special place in my heart, and I love all of them in my own way because each grandchild is a blessing from the Lord in his or her unique way.

As I said before, I love all of my eight grandchildren, and I am their Oma. I have the right and duty to spoil each one. Did I say eight? Yes, I have eight wonderful grandchildren because my daughter gave birth to a sweet little girl not long ago, and she and Troy gave her the name Ariel. I think my daughter felt blessed by the Lord when Ariel arrived. Everyone loves the little one, and she is growing up in a wonderful family. She has to fight two boys who tease her and take things away from her, and she will not step back. Both boys love Ariel, and Ariel loves the boys.

Jacob is the one who makes everyone laugh, and he loves to watch the wildlife. Manny is very artistic, and when I use only a pen and paper to write, he uses paper and all kinds of colors to sketch to draw and create amazing pictures. He also likes to use his imagination to draw cartoon characters and animals.

Katie and Jessie also love their little sister Ariel very much. Katie likes to write and sing, and she has a beautiful voice (just like her mom). Jessie writes poetry, and I think she might write her own book one day. Jessie also has a beautiful voice, and when I look at Jessie, I can see a prayer the Lord answered in His own way.

Children and grandchildren are a gift to treasure forever and ever. Without God and His love for the world, we wouldn't have any children. I will not write very much about my children and grandchildren and their life. I think I will give each one the opportunity to write their story. I hope that the Lord will give me enough time to enjoy all of my children and grandchildren, and I hope that I helped them to have faith and trust in the Lord, because that is the main reason for me to write. The Lord is giving me all the words I need to write because I had forgotten many things; the Lord helped me to remember. I think if we only believe in His word and power, we would have no problem facing any situation and mastering all difficulties. Without the Lord and His daily guidance we are nothing. Regardless who we are and where we are, God will be with us if we trust Him and reach out to Him. We can talk to the Lord anytime and He will answer us. Sometimes we do not like His answer, but if we trust Him and give it all to Him, we will receive the greatest gift from the Lord: *His unconditional love!*

With His love we also receive peace and comfort. It is never easy when we lose a child, a parent, or a friend. Death is the end of our life on Earth, and no one can escape death. Everyone on this earth will die one day. This is a fact! God is the One and only One who knows when our time on Earth is over, and when He calls us, all we have to do is take His hand. For a dead person, pain and suffering on Earth is over, and only the people who are close will feel angry, lonely and a deep pain in their heart. If we believe in Jesus and ask the Lord to help us, comfort us and give us peace in our hearts and minds, He will be right on our side, and we can feel His holy and wonderful presence. Nothing, *absolutely nothing*, is impossible for God! He will never ask us to pay or to call back. He gives us His answer and works in mysterious ways.

We don't have to say words out loud. We don't have to learn the scripture and remember word by word. Even if we could remember all the words in the Holy Bible but didn't believe in Jesus—that He is God's only son who took the cross for the world to save us—we wouldn't hear God. We would walk in the dark and Satan would have no problem to take over. I have asked myself so many times why we have so much evil in this world and why God allows it. The answer is God gives us a choice to follow Him and to trust and obey Him.

Satan will always try to stop us calling on God and fill our minds with earthly things. It is true that most people will reach out for money, power, and an easy life on Earth. Who needs the Bible? Who needs God? Who knows if there is even a God? Have you seen Him? God and Jesus are only for children, and I am an adult and can do what I want. I like my life, and I want it to be rich and have all the power on Earth over the people. I am famous, and I love what I am doing. It is fun to see others suffer because they want to be good and love God, so they would rather be poor and sit in their church and pray to a God who is not real. God is a fairy tale, and it is told many times by famous and outstanding scientists. It was also scientifically proven to the people that this world was a rock, and it exploded millions of years ago, and this explosion created rivers, mountains, and deep, blue seas. It was a chemical reaction and this is how the earth was created. If people don't believe in God, they will be happy to pass on this so-called scientific proof about the creation of this world.

But this sounds more like a fairy tale to me, and I have only one question: who made the rock? God is the only One who created this world out of nothing but His command. Everything turned out to be beautiful and perfect until He put us in the garden, and until we the people began to question His creation, reaching out for more and more. Hate, anger, and envy took over, and we the people began to kill and destroy each other because we became what Satan wanted us to be: unbelievers.

God was ready to destroy everything and put an end to all of it, but He saved us and gave us another chance. He sent His only son to save us, and Jesus shed His blood and died for us on the cross. He cried out to God when He was on the cross, "Father, forgive them because they know not what they do!"

He saved the world with His blood! What a price to pay! All we have to do is follow Him and believe. Love one another and have peace on Earth. It would be so easy, but Satan uses his power and puts doubt into the people. Everyone who follows the evil spirit will have power, fame and wealth, because that is what is important to the world. Satan lost when he tried to convince Jesus, and he also lost when other people gave it all to the Lord and were not willing to deny Him for a better life on Earth—in richness, power, and fame.

God knows our heart and our mind, and He knows our deepest dreams and secrets. I can tell from my own experience that God was the only one who knew my deepest wish I had buried in my heart, and no one in my family knew it. I never talked about it to a single person or anyone in my family—only to God and to Jesus in my prayers. God fulfilled my wish, and He did it in a way I never expected.

I was still living in Roosevelt, and Ricky was just two years old when I decided to follow the Lord's call to be baptized in a small pond outside of Roosevelt. It was a wonderful, unforgettable moment when I walked into the water, and when the pastor submerged me under the water, I felt a tremendous touch to my heart. When I opened my eyes and saw the blue sky and the golden sunlight, the pastor said that this was the same way the Lord Jesus Christ was baptized in the Jordan River in Israel.

I looked up to the sky, and I felt an unexplainable desire to walk where Jesus once walked when He was on this earth, but I didn't speak a word to anyone and locked the wish up in my heart. I said to myself that this was impossible because I would never be able to pay for a trip to Israel. I would not be able to pay for any trip because we had just enough to pay for the farm business and to take care of the family. When I went home with my children, Ricky told Dennis, "Mommy went in the water, but she is okay; the man pulled her out."

I told my husband that I went to be baptized, but this was not the same. It was very touching. We never talked about it again, and I had started to write my first English poetry because to me it was like talking to the Lord. I also felt His presence when I wrote a poem. I don't know how many poems I wrote, but I wrote all of my poems only to give God the honor and glory. World of Poetry published some of my poems, and I also wrote some poems to give to other people. When God gives us a gift, He wants us to share it with others, and poetry is a gift from God, so I never kept my poems for myself. I know that some of my poems helped people to reach out to the Lord.

My first poem I wrote when I was out in the field on the tractor all by myself. I always had a pen in my pocket, and I took from a seed sack a paper and began to write the first lines down. When I went home, I wrote more. Soon I was writing anytime, and I was able to face daily problems much easier. It also helped me to learn the language so I was able to understand people and to communicate with others. In the beginning it was not easy, but eventually I got used to all the difficulties, and my English/German dictionary became the most important book for me. I still use it and will not go anyplace without it.

I think it is very important to understand and to speak the language of the country you live in. I grew up in Germany, and the language I spoke was German. When I moved to the United States and decided to live in America and become an American citizen, I needed to learn the language and customs. But I was also very surprised when I picked up the phone and heard the operator telling me, *if you like to speak in English, please press 1*. Why? I was in America, and English was the language. Why do I have to press a number to speak in English? Well, I think I will never understand it. I have learned over the years to stand firm for the things I believe, and even if I had to stand all by myself, I was never alone because the Lord was always guiding me. He carried me when I was unable to walk anymore.

When I had spinal meningitis, I lost most of my hearing, and it was very difficult for me to understand. One day I went to visit my daughter, and I watched a Christian TV program with her, and I heard the pastor talking about a coming event in Minneapolis. He invited everyone to hear the wonderful Gospel of Jesus Christ and to feel His healing touch. My daughter had planned to attend this meeting and had made some arrangements for a bus ride to the cities. She decided not to go; instead, she wanted me to go. I also had a friend who wanted to go to this special event. We went, and my friend Lorraine knew I had no money to pay for anything, so she had paid for the hotel stay and all expenses in advance.

This trip was unforgettable for me. We didn't check into the hotel; instead, we joined the crowd and waited in line at the Target Center. When the doors opened, more than sixteen thousand people were singing and praising God the Lord. Pastor Benny was standing in the light on the stage. I knew he had a message for me. He lifted his hands and looked up and shouted, "There is power in the mighty name of Jesus, and He will pour out His Holy Spirit because nothing, absolutely nothing, is impossible tonight if you put your trust and faith in God the Almighty!"

Pastor Benny stopped. His voice was very quiet, and with a tremble, he said, "Ladies and gentlemen, I've come to Minneapolis, Minnesota because Jesus is walking into the place here tonight. Jesus will do a miracle for each and every one of you. Right now, right here in the Target Center of Minneapolis, because He knows Minnesota needs Jesus Christ!"

This night was the night where Jesus called people to trust Him, believe in His healing power, and listen to the holy words. I think anyone who also attended the crusade will tell you that these were unforgettable moments. People who came in a wheelchair could walk and left the chair behind. This was real and not staged because we had met some people before, and we knew about their problems and their long struggle of being unable to walk. By the power of God, they got out of their wheelchairs and walked. "Fire and Touch!" Pastor Benny screamed.

The crowd tumbled, and many went on the floor. People were anointed by God's Holy Spirit. Pastor Benny pounded his fist on the podium and began to rebuke all kinds of sickness in the name of Jesus. I could feel the power and the presence of the Lord. It was God who healed, not the pastor. It was Jesus who did the miracles, not Pastor Benny. It was the Holy Spirit that had touched us.

I felt the Lord's touch, and I gave it all to Him and trusted Him that He would help me find a job and have better hearing. I knew when Pastor Benny prayed and asked the Lord to touch me that my whole life would change. Soon I would have enough to do what God wanted me to do with my life, and I would find a job to take care of everything. But before I left the stage, Pastor Benny called me back and told me that the Lord gave him a message to pass on to me. He said, "You will soon walk where our wonderful Lord Jesus Christ walked."

I was very surprised because this was my unspoken wish. How was it really possible that Pastor Benny knew about this? How could he say that I would go to Israel? I was very surprised, and to tell you the truth, I really didn't believe that I would ever be able to make a trip to the Holy Land. But deep in my heart I felt a joy, and I had the desire more and more to walk where our wonderful Lord and Savior walked.

When I left the stage, I was able to hear and I thanked the Lord, but my thoughts went to the last message the pastor gave me, and I was unable to forget about it. I became a prayer warrior for Pastor Benny, and I asked the Lord in my prayer to give me peace, patience and faith. I contacted the ministry, and many people prayed with me and everyone thanked the Lord for sending me to the Holy Land. But before the Lord answered my prayers, He gave me a dream and I saw a beautiful banner in blue with the words *Mighty Warrior of Jesus* on a huge shield with a sword. In the middle of the shield was a silver dove; she was holding the earth. I thought this was awesome, and I said, "Oh Lord, this is great."

The hand of the Lord was holding the banner and the Lord told me, "Make it!"

I woke up and cried. I still had the picture of the banner in my mind and wrote the words down. I couldn't sleep anymore, and I prayed and told the Lord that I was not able to do it. I could sew, but I couldn't draw. But I heard His words again: "Make it!"

I went to town and stopped at a store to see if I could find some material for a banner. When I entered the store, I saw the same bright blue velvet, and I purchased it. I also found silver sequins and pearls for the letters and picture.

I had all the material and took it to the church basement. I don't remember how many times I tried to draw a dove holding the earth. After I tried and tried, I went in front of the altar on my knees and cried, "Lord, You want me to make this banner, but I can't draw. Give me someone to do it or You need to draw it."

I heard the Lord telling me to trust Him and to take the pen and draw. Before I could say anything, the pencil in my hand had drawn a beautiful dove holding the earth. I know that the Lord drew the picture. The Lord also helped me to make the banner, and over the next weeks, I went every day to the church to work on it.

After four weeks, the banner was finished, and I gave it to the church. The pastor wanted to pay for the material, but I knew the Lord wanted me to take care of it.

When I was still working on the banner, I made remarks to some friends that I would never again be able to make another banner, and if I had to do it over again, I wouldn't use velvet for it because it was very difficult to do. Soon I found out it was not a good idea to make a statement like that because the Lord was in charge, and He was the designer, not I. So, the Lord gave me another dream with another banner. It was red velvet with a cross, a crown of thorns, a crown of glory, a dove, a fish, three golden rings, four nails, and the words, *For God so loved the world that He gave His only begotten son that whosoever believes in Him should not perish but have everlasting life.* It was a beautiful banner, and the Lord told me again to make it.

When I went to the same store, I could see a bright red, soft velvet on the wall. I asked the lady about it, and she told me this was the only velvet available because at this time of the year many customers buy velvet for Christmas. It was only a few weeks till Christmas. I bought the velvet, and I knew I needed to get all the material and special sequins and pearls to make the banner. I told the lady I needed to make the banner for our church and that the Lord had given me all the details in my dream. I had not very much money, so if I needed to pay more, I would have to come back later. But the lady told me she would give me everything I needed, and if I didn't have enough to pay for it, she would pay the rest. She said, "If the Lord tells you to do some special work for Him, you have to do it."

I had enough to pay for everything, and I thanked the Lord for his wonderful answers to my prayers.

When I entered the church, I felt the Holy Spirit was in the church, and He was guiding my hands to make a banner. It was designed by the Lord, and I know that the Lord would help me do everything right. He gave me a wonderful person, and she helped me cut out letters and keep everything perfect and straight.

After we had the cross outlined and attached the words, I bought four big nails and fastened it on each side of the cross on the top, put three golden rings on one side, and the crown of glory on the other side. We attached the fish and the peace dove to the banner, and my friend told me that it was done; we had it finished just in time.

I looked at the banner and I thought something was missing. I went to the Lord and prayed, and when I looked up, I saw the crown of thorns, and I knew I needed to put the crown of thorns on top of the cross. I went outside and it was cold, but I cut branches with thorns from a rosebush and made a crown to attach over the cross on the banner. Now it was finished, and I thanked the Lord for using me and giving me all the help and guidance to make two beautiful banners for His glory and honor. I gave both banners to our church, and I know the church still has them.

When the Lord touches us and talks to us, we need to trust Him and listen to His word. We can't question the Lord. I have learned when you only trust people you will suffer a lot and will be disappointed and hurt. God will never ever hurt us because He loves us unconditionally—no strings attached!

After I finished the two banners, God gave me another dream. I was in my dream in a strange land, and I was walking a stony street. I heard a voice talking to me, and I saw many people. I was unable to stand still. I was trying to talk, but it was impossible. I cried and felt pain all over my body. I had bloody hands and feet, but someone lifted me up, and I stopped crying because I felt peace and love filling my heart and mind. I heard music and saw a beautiful river and many people in the river, and I also walked into the water. When I woke up, I knew the dream was a message from the Lord. Soon I found the answer, and it was a surprise to my family and friends when I received a check for the exact amount I needed to book a trip to the Holy Land—to walk where our Lord Jesus Christ walked, lived, and died on the cross for our sins.

Immediately, I contacted the ministry and told them that I would be able to visit the Holy Land. We prayed and thanked the Lord for answering my prayers and making it possible for me to walk where Jesus walked, and to achieve the full experience of the Gospel. I know today that the trip to Israel had a tremendous effect on my life, and I am so thankful that I was able to visit and stand with many others on the holy ground in Israel.

To this day, I still have no clue who sent the check, but I know that God was in charge. All I did was praise and worship Him, and I never questioned the Lord's wonderful miracles.

20

Unforgettable Trip to Israel

At the time I made all the arrangements for my trip, I didn't know how much my life would change. I had traveled many times, and at first I thought this trip was in many ways the same as my previous trips to different places in the country or overseas. But I soon found out it was much more. The flight from New York to Tel Aviv took about fourteen hours. When I arrived with many others in Tel Aviv-Jaffa airport, I could feel joy and love begin to come over me. We all got picked up by buses and brought to a hotel in Tiberias; it is located on the western shore of the Sea of Galilee. It was our first stop, and when I entered the hotel lobby, I joined several people who went on their knees to thank the Lord for making it possible to visit the Holy Land. It was late when I finally went to sleep. We were told that we would be starting early to begin our journey to all the places where our wonderful Lord Jesus Christ was born, lived, and died for us.

Our day started with a great breakfast in the hotel restaurant. We were told to enjoy everything and also feel free to pack a bag with Jewish bread and fruit for the first trip on a special bus assigned to us. It was a long ride, and we were all glad that we had packed a bag with delicious fruit, cheese, and bread.

The bus brought us to the ruins of the ancient city of Caesarea by the sea, which used to be the headquarters of the Roman administration. Two gigantic Roman statues dated from the third century AD—one in red igneous rock and one in white marble—were well preserved.

Our next stop was Megiddo, also known as the bloodiest spot on Earth because no place on Earth had seen so many battles. The Hebrew word for Megiddo is well known; it means Armageddon. It is

Israel's valley, a vast area in the heart of the Holy Land. We went all the way up a hill, and we could see far out stretching twenty-five miles by fourteen miles—from Mt. Tabor in the north to the foothills of Mt. Gilboa, then to the base of Mt. Carmel, and from Mt. Carmel back to Tabor. The well-known valley of Megiddo is triangular in shape. A huge water tunnel that had brought fresh water into the city is still well preserved. The city of Megiddo overlooks the valley of Megiddo.

Our next point on the map through the Holy Land would be Nazareth, and we were all very excited because it was the hometown of Jesus, and it was the place of the annunciation by the angel Gabriel to Mary—that she would bear a child of the Holy Spirit. This place was marked by a big church built in 1936.

From Nazareth we went to Cana, where Jesus had performed His first miracles when He turned water into wine. In Nain, Jesus raised a widow's son from the dead.

We went back to Tiberias, and the special miracle service was unforgettable. It was held by the Sea of Galilee. We also visited Capernaum where Jesus preached for the first time, healed many people, and raised a young girl from the dead. Tabgha was the place where Jesus multiplied the loaves and fishes to feed the multitude during His Sermon on the Mount where He gave The Beatitudes.

We also went on a very special, two-hour boat ride on the Sea of Galilee and had Saint-Peter fish with Jewish bread and a huge order of french fries. It was here where Jesus walked on the water. This sea is indeed unpredictable. When we started out, there was beautiful sunshine, but we went through a big change of weather, and after a short time, we hit a heavy storm. It is a fact that the Sea of Galilee suffers from very sudden and severe storms. Within minutes, it can turn from being very calm and clear, to a raging sea with waves up to fourteen and fifteen feet high. I also enjoyed the feast. The fish was delicious, and you could eat the whole fish with the head and tail, served of course with the Jewish bread, and this was also very special.

We had a great time, and this was our last day in Tiberias, but before we went on this wonderful boat ride, we were all ready to follow the Lord's call, and it was very special. Because we would soon leave, and it would be our last day at the hotel in Tiberias on the Sea of Galilee, this was the most important moment for me. It was the day we were all ready to attend a baptismal service and be baptized in the same river where Jesus was baptized by John the Baptist. It is called Yardenit, and it means "baptismal site." I will never forget this day. This was the most wonderful moment in my life—when I walked into the river and the pastor submerged me under the water. I felt touched by the Lord, and I knew at this moment that my life would belong to God. I gave it all to Him. Yes, I was baptized in the Jordan River, and it was true, not a dream. God had told me that I would be baptized in Israel, and God kept His promise.

We stayed at the hotel on the Sea of Galilee five nights and left early in the morning. Then our special bus took us to Jerusalem. We were staying in a very nice hotel, and from there we went to another special place every day. Jerusalem is the heart of Israel, and as important as Jerusalem is, the cities and towns around Jerusalem are also very significant—because nearby is the town of Bethlehem where our wonderful Lord Jesus was born, and the town of Bethany is also nearby. This was the place where Jesus raised Lazarus from the dead.

We visited the Mount of Olives, the place where Jesus' ascension was. The Mount of Olives will also be the place for the Lord's second coming. The Garden of Gethsemane is on the slopes of the Mount of Olives, and this was the place where Jesus went in agony and prayed to His father on the night of His arrest, when Judas betrayed Jesus, and the disciples deserted Him. The garden was very well taken care of, and the olive trees were very big. We were told that eight ancient olive trees may date to the first century AD and probably grew from the roots of the very trees among which our Lord Jesus Christ prayed. In the Garden of Gethsemane is the Church of All Nations, and many believe that the olive trees on the church's grounds are more than two thousand years old and might be the same trees under which Jesus spend his final night.

More than twenty-five churches from different denominations were built close by and on the Mount of Olives. We visited the Pater Noster Church where you could read the Lord's Prayer in fifty different languages inscribed on its walls. Inside the church was a small cave and it was believed that this was the site where Jesus taught His disciples to pray. When I touched one of the huge trees, I felt a tremendous pain in my heart, and I passed out and fell down. One of the people came and helped me get up. Her name was Claudia, and we became best friends; to this day we are still in touch.

After we visited the Garden of Gethsemane, we were told that the bus would bring us to a special place close to the Mount of Olives for a special "This is your day" television taping. Pastor Benny gave a wonderful message to all, and we worshiped and glorified the Lord Jesus Christ. The rest of the day we could go on our own, and we all went to explore the old stores, buying souvenirs and postcards.

The hotel was ready to spoil us with a great meal. It was November 12, and our next stop was Bethlehem. It was not the same, and we could see many people were not very friendly. Little kids threw rocks at the bus, and our guide could not leave the bus to visit the city of Bethlehem with us, because it is against the law for any Israelite to enter Bethlehem or any city located in Palestine. Bethlehem belongs to Palestine, and we saw many soldiers in the city.

We went to the Church of Nativity and walked to the hall of the Basilica of Nativity. Everyone had to wait in line, and only a handful of visitors could enter the Holy Grotto of the Nativity, one at the time, because it was a very narrow stairway; we had to have much patience. When I stood on the place in the Grotto, I was glad I waited because it was such a wonderful experience to stand close to the place where Jesus was born and where it all began. I also can't forget the feeling I had when I was standing in front of a huge marble floor with the star of Bethlehem surrounded by many oil lamps and candles.

Before we left Bethlehem, we visited the Milk Grotto; it was the Grotto where Mary, Joseph, and the infant Jesus temporarily took shelter as they fled to Egypt during Herod's slaughter of the innocents. It was a very small place and had an altar with candles and flowers.

The Shepherd's Field and Shepherd's Field Church were our next stops. The church was built where the angel announced the Good News to shepherds in the field, that Jesus Christ was born in Bethlehem—that He was the Messiah, the Son of God! The shepherds left their sheep and went to see the baby. They saw the star and followed it to the place where the newborn King was.

After our visit in the city of Bethlehem, we went back to Jerusalem, and this was a very emotional moment for me because we went to the old city of Jerusalem. We visited all the special historic places of Old Jerusalem. It is a compact city and enclosed with an ancient wall. It is said that Jerusalem was the capital of Israel yesterday, is the capital of Israel today, and will be the capital of the world tomorrow. God gave the world ten measures of beauty—nine in Jerusalem and one to the rest of the world.

The center of the world is Israel. The center of Israel is the city of Jerusalem. The center of Jerusalem was the Temple. The center of the Temple was the Holy of Holies. The center of the Holy of Holies was the Ark of the Covenant. The walls of the Old City of Jerusalem embrace history and have thirty-five towers and eight gates. It is significant that to this day the city is still encompassed by walls and gates. But it is also in the Bible prophecy: "God says that Jerusalem's gates are everlasting."

We visited only a few gates. One of them is called the Lion's Gate and is located on the eastern wall—the entrance to the Via Dolorosa, which means "way of suffering." The Damascus Gate faces to the north towards the city of Damascus. It is the most-used gate. The Zion Gate faces south to Mt. Zion, and is so narrow that a car has difficulty passing through it. The Jaffa Gate is well known and located in the western wall. The opening of this gate reunited East and West

Jerusalem. Herod's palace was by this gate, and David's tower is here. But the most famous and most talked-about gate in Jerusalem is the Golden Gate. This gate is on the east side and it is a double gate. This is the gate our Lord Jesus Christ used over two thousand years ago when He rode on a donkey for His triumphal entry into Jerusalem.

When the Mohammedans heard that a king of Israel was to enter by this gate, they were afraid and sealed and blocked the gate. We all went to the western wall, and this was very intense because there were many people praying, singing, and crying out to their God. Many wrote words on paper and put it in small openings in the wall. We were told to do the same and to tell the Lord our deepest desire.

I can't remember how many people put notes in the wall, but I remember that I was fascinated by the Temple Mount marked by the Dome of the Rock, which is also the most picturesque and historic spot in Jerusalem—and maybe in the entire world. It was here where Abraham was ready to sacrifice his son Isaac. It was Herod's Temple where Jesus went when he was only twelve years old. It was also the same temple where Jesus got angry and kicked out the money changers and healed a lame man. The Dome of the Rock stands in the Temple Mount on Mount Moriah. Herod's Temple was destroyed after Jesus died, and this was the fulfilling of the prophecy Jesus had made concerning the temple's destruction. The present Dome of the Rock is now a Muslim place of worship, and it is one of the oldest structures standing in the Old City of Jerusalem.

The top of the dome is covered with a layer of gold leaf. The Muslims believe that Mohammed was sent to Heaven from the rock inside the dome, and Jerusalem is to be considered one of the most sacred cities in the Muslim world besides Mecca and Medina. The Muslims also believe that Mohammed will come back with Jesus, He will assist Mohammed in Jerusalem to determine the fate of the souls, and the resurrection of the dead will be near the Dome of the Rock.

We also visited the place where Jesus was tried and scourged, and we saw etchings on the stony floor. It was a game, and we were informed it was used by Roman soldiers using prisoners as mock kings in a life-and-death game or match. It was the place where Jesus was mocked on these same pavement stones. The Arch designates the spot where Pilate declared, "Behold the man."

Outside by the Zion Gate is the Palace of Caiaphas—he was the high priest when Jesus was tried, and it was also the place where Peter denied Jesus three times before the cock's crow. The Church of Cock Crowing commemorates this event.

Before we went to the next place in Jerusalem, we went to a special spot where our whole bus group posed for a nice picture with the golden Dome of the Rock in the background. It was a beautiful day, and we all needed to wear sun glasses because the sun was very bright. I forgot to bring my glasses, and I had to wear a hat to cover my eyes.

Soon we would be on our way back to the United States, and we had no idea when we came back to the hotel in Jerusalem that we were all invited to a special farewell dinner. After the dinner, we had another surprise, and one of the guests stood up and gave a great performance playing the Ram's Horn, also known as Shofars. He did an excellent job, and it was very special.

The next day was very special too, and we went to Qumran, the city of salt. The city is famous because it is the place where the Dead Sea Scrolls were found in almost perfectly preserved copies of the Old Testament.

The Dead Sea, or salt sea, is the saltiest in the world. I walked into the sea, and I was floating in the water because the salt water made it impossible to sink. We had a great time, and I enjoyed floating in the water of the Dead Sea.

Before we left we could also ride on a Camel. Camels are still being used in the desert. I had very much fun sitting and riding on a camel, after I saw that I didn't have to be afraid of them.

The last day in Israel brought us back to the gates of the Old City of Jerusalem. We visited the Upper Room where Jesus had the

Last Supper with His disciples and revealed to them that one of them would betray Him soon. This was also the place where the Lord told Peter that he would deny Him three times. When I entered the Upper Room, I again felt a terrible pain in my heart, and I had a difficult time standing up. My thoughts went to the Lord, and tears filled my eyes. How much did our Lord Jesus suffer when He gave bread and wine to Judas, who would soon hand Him over to the soldiers with a kiss to be beaten, tortured, and crucified? I don't think we really know how much the Son of God suffered for our sins.

We left the Upper Room, and our guide gave us some advice for the next visit. It was specifically for our safety because we saw many people begging us and asking for money. It was also a good idea not to pay the posted price for souvenirs right away. Instead, we needed to try to get a better deal, and we should never walk alone. It was another moment for me where I needed my friend's help because when we walked the Via Dolorosa, I had a difficult time keeping up with the group. Every step up the hill on the old rocky street was extremely painful, and I began to cry. I saw many people who were carrying a cross on their shoulders, and I could believe that our wonderful Lord Jesus Christ suffered a lot, because on both sides of the Via Dolorosa were buildings, and the people had no problem mocking Him, laughing at Him, pushing Him, and hurting Him more. It was not easy to walk on this road. The name Via Dolorosa means "way of suffering," because it is a fact that Jesus walked this road and had to carry a heavy cross. He had received a terrible beating beforehand and was already in crucial pain and agony.

The street is marked fourteen times. The first two markings are actually inside the tower, and the last five markings are inside the Church of the Holy Sepulchre. These markings, or stations, were established in the fourteenth century. Station one: Jesus is tried and condemned to die. Station two: Jesus receives the Cross. Station three: Jesus falls down for the first time. Station four: Jesus meets His mother. Station five: Simon takes and caries the cross for Jesus. Station six: the woman wipes the sweat from the face of Jesus. Station seven: Jesus falls down the second time. Station eight: Jesus consoles the women of Jerusalem. Station nine: Jesus falls down the third time. Station ten: Jesus is stripped of His garments. Station eleven: Jesus is nailed to the cross. Station twelve: Jesus dies on the cross. Station thirteen: Jesus' body is removed from the cross. Lastly, station fourteen: Jesus' body is laid in the tomb. I had a very difficult time, but I needed to walk the Via Dolorosa, and it was not easy.

After we went back to the hotel, we had to get ready for our trip back to the USA. I decided to go with a group of friends to buy some souvenirs and postcards. I was not sure what to get, but when I saw things made out of olive wood, I purchased a Nativity set with a hand-carved stable, stars, the baby Jesus, Mary, Joseph, a shepherd, sheep, the three kings, and an angel. I was very happy that I found such a beautiful set, and it is today for me a treasure from the Holy Land! It is a wonderful reminder of unforgettable days in my life. Yes, the Nativity set was hand carved by a person in Israel, and I made the decision to purchase it. I can look at it all the time, and on Christmas I place it under our tree.

But the trip to the Holy Land was much more for me. I know to this day that it was God who made it possible for me to walk in the footsteps of our wonderful Lord Jesus Christ! He heard my unspoken prayer and answered in His way. He carved every moment of the ten days in Israel deep in my heart. Israel—*I will remember forever!* It was more than a trip; it was an answer. It was proof that God is in charge of my life and keeps all of His promises.

21

A New Chapter and New Friends, Don and Cheri

God gives us all a choice to hear His voice and command to follow Him. I know that many people only call on God when they are in danger and fear fills their heart. I also know that people who don't believe in the Lord will tell others, when the danger is over, that they were very lucky, instead of saying to the whole world that God took over, answered their cry, and saved their life. Sometimes I feel that people are afraid to let others know they believe in Jesus Christ because they think it is much better to tell everyone that they were very lucky when they got hit by a car or when a tornado roared to the land and took the life of others. I asked a friend of mine why he said that he was lucky when he was in a very bad car accident and three people died. His answer was, "Well, what would you call it? I was lucky because I could have died, so I call myself lucky."

I looked at him and said, "Have you ever thought that maybe the Lord saved you?"

He laughed and told me, "I am an adult, and Jesus Christ is not here; He is dead. And besides, who knows that He is real? I believed in Him when I was a child, and I don't know why because I have never seen Him. I think all that is just a fairy tale and is used by parents to make children behave. But adults know better, and they know that there are lucky and not-so-lucky people, and I tell you I was lucky."

Well, my friend became very sick shortly after the "lucky" accident and I visited him in the hospital. I hardly recognized him, and he was in much pain. He took my hand and said, "Alusru, will you pray for me and ask the Lord to let me die? I think you have a better connection to Him. Besides, I am a man, and God might not listen to a man like me, so I think it is better if a woman talks to Him."

I fell on my knees, put my arms around him, and told him that God was holding him and that He loves him very much. I also told him that only God made the decision when life is over, and we have no right to tell the Lord what to do because He is in charge of each life. I prayed with my friend, and I closed my prayer with the same words Opa used: *Lord, not my will but Your will be done.*

My friend did not die and lived for over twenty years, but when he left the hospital he was not the same anymore because he was unable to walk and could only speak a few words. He became very close to the Lord, and when he was pulled out of his easy life and ended up in a wheelchair, he reached out to the Lord, and the Lord gave him His hand and told him to follow Him and to trust Him. The only words he could say without any problems were, "Jesus, I love you! Jesus, I thank you! Amen."

Even though my friend was unable to talk or walk and needed others to go on with his life, he became a follower of Jesus Christ and became a living testimony for many people. I was staying in touch with him and also with his mom. When I left Germany, I missed Rusty, but he told me in his way that God wanted me to stay in America. His mom sent me a picture Rusty drew for me, and it was like a message. It had two crosses: one cross was in bright, golden light; from the other cross came tears, and it was broken. On top of the broken cross was a white dove. I wanted to ask Rusty why he drew that picture, but when I contacted his mom, she told me that Rusty was with the Lord. He told her to tell me that Jesus loves me. He would be with me and comfort me soon. I thought at first that Rusty was telling me that he was soon going to be with Jesus, but when my sweet little baby Ricky died, I knew this was the message Rusty had given me. I told his mom all the wonderful answers the Lord gave me. I visited with her when I went to see my mom in Germany, and I also visited the parents of Sylvia, my godchild.

I became Sylvia's godmother shortly after I became a midwife. She was very special. She became a beautiful mom, and her husband loved her very much. They had two boys, and when Sylvia was just twenty-four, she was diagnosed with leukemia. She died just before she turned twenty-five. Her parents took care of the boys because Sylvia's husband died in a terrible car accident. I shared with Sylvia's parents all the things that happened in my life here in the United States, and I told them that I know the pain in the heart when a child dies, but if we give it all to Jesus and let Him be in charge of our pain, He will hold us and comfort us and soon we will understand. When God gives us a load, He also gives us angels to help us carry it.

I told this to many friends and strangers. I had to be very strong when God took my mom home, and a year later, he called Dennis home to be with Him and Ricky. Dennis and I had our ups and downs, but he knew I was very close to the Lord. When we had many problems, he thought it would be a good solution to get a divorce, but I told him that I would not agree to a divorce because it would not solve any problems. Besides, I promised to be his wife till death do us part, and I didn't believe God wanted us to break up our marriage.

He went to get some answers, contacted a lawyer, and found out it wasn't that easy. I believe most people give up much too fast, and in most cases they are angry and unwilling to negotiate with each other. It is also very easy here in the United States to get a divorce in a short time, and I think the ones who suffer most are the children. In no time, a wonderful family with dreams and plans for the future is shattered in pieces.

I can tell you I suffered a lot when my parents got a divorce, but it was not because they were unfaithful to each other; it was because my dad became ill and was on all kinds of drugs, and it was also very easy for his mother to make all kinds of statements against my mom because she never liked her or us children. My dad believed his mother and accused my mom of being unfaithful. He also physically abused her and came home with other women. I know my mom tried to stay with him. They were married for thirty-three years when my mom signed the divorce papers. Shortly after, my dad committed suicide.

I always loved Dad, and I was heartbroken when he came home with other women, and when he abused Mom. I could not stand by and let him do all this to Mom, so I tried to talk to him, but I was not successful. Too much damage was done, and Dad told me that he loved the other woman. All he wanted to do was marry her, but Mom would not sign the paper. I knew the other woman was waiting for my dad to die so she would get his pension. It didn't work for her, so she put Dad into a nursing home, and shortly after, dad killed himself.

I know Dad was very much in love with Mom, and they went to all kinds of places. Dad surprised Mom every year with flowers and special gifts, but when Dad walked away from the Lord, he changed, and a marriage of thirty-three years fell into Satan's hand. He took over.

I believe some of you might not like what I said about divorce. Sometimes it is the only answer, because when both parties are unfaithful to each other, it is better to walk away and start a new relationship. Another reason is when there is some kind of abuse— mental or physical—it is better to put a stop to it because it can get ugly and can also put the children in danger. God doesn't want you to stay in a marriage with adultery and abuse. If you both love the Lord and trust the Lord, Satan can't destroy the family ties. But if one walks away from God, any marriage starts to fall apart. When my dad went to the court to make my mom sign the divorce papers, he lost because the judge asked my dad how many years he was married to Mom. When he said twenty-nine years, the judge denied the divorce.

He said, "She was good to you for over twenty-eight years. Now you want to marry a younger woman. Come back after five years. Divorce is denied!"

Although my mom won, she was very much in pain, and I could feel some of it. Mom began to change. She was often very depressed, and when I tried to talk to her she would look at me with tears in her eyes and would tell me not to ask her any more questions because this was between her and my dad. So I didn't have much to say, but I said, "Mom, you both love God! God can change it. Why didn't you let Him?"

I still can remember Mom's answer and her face when she said, "Your dad walked out and the door is closed. All I will ask Jesus is to hold me in His arms. I know He will, and I have asked Him to forgive your dad. I am so thankful that Opa and my mom never saw all this. My mom loved your dad, and Opa was happy that your dad and I were married. It would be devastating for both to witness the broken pieces and the divorce."

I know it was very hard on all of us, and so I had no other choice. I had to let it be, and shortly after my dad moved out from the home, I went to the United States and married Dennis. When I was pregnant with Pam, my dad made the request to see his first grandchild, and I was not willing to do it. I know it was not the right decision, and I had no right to say no. This was payback, and I know it was wrong, but I was so angry at my dad and I did not ask the Lord. I was happy to fire back at my dad: "You see? That is what you get when you hurt us and when you walk away from Mom! You will never see or hold your grandchildren!"

Today I feel bad that I was so full of anger and hate. I didn't ask the Lord to make a decision because I wanted to punish my dad. But this is what anger and hate can do to a person when God is left out. We say that a marriage is only between two people, but I learned that a good marriage is between God, one man, and one woman. God will bless the marriage, and it will be a happy marriage. Without God, a marriage soon becomes weak and brittle and might end in a painful divorce. In most cases, a divorce will destroy everything, and children suffer for a very long time, especially when the children are very young and can't understand why Daddy is gone, since in most divorce cases the children will live with their mom. Sometimes they will never see Daddy again.

I can still remember when I called out to my dad when I had a problem, and then I realized that he was gone and I had to solve problems by myself. I tried to let things go and forget the time I missed my dad, but it is almost impossible because he took care of us when our family was intact, and Dad surprised my mom many times with flowers and little gifts. I know my mom loved Dad, and she took care of him when he was diagnosed with early-stage cancer in his thyroid. Cancer was treated with a heavy amount of radiation through needles inserted into the thyroid. I remember that Mom was often very sick when she came home after visiting Dad at the hospital. She was exposed to radiation, because we didn't have any specific restrictions or regulations for visitors who came to visit a patient receiving radiation treatment. Today, no one is permitted to enter any area where radium is. The patient is totally isolated from everyone.

I know Mom and Dad suffered a lot, and when Dad had to be on heavy drugs, he lost all control over his life, and it made him angry and furious. When Dad was released from the hospital, he went to visit his mom, and she saw a chance to destroy my parents' marriage. She knew Dad loved Mom, but she also knew that he was jealous. Jealousy is the reason for many divorces, and it will destroy everything.

When Dad came home, he started to abuse Mom because he was jealous, and also had found out from his mother that Mom had an affair with another man when he was in the hospital. Mom never had an affair; she was always faithful and tried every way to make Dad happy and help him during the time he was so sick. When we had many bills because of Dad's sickness, Mom went to work. When we were gone and out of the house, my dad abused Mom, and all the love he had for her was gone. He was beating her and mentally abusing her, and my brothers and I had no idea what was going on. I had seen some bruises on Mom when I came home visiting, but Mom told me that she hurt herself at work. I had no reason not to believe her. All I had seen was that Mom was often very tired, and most of the time Dad was not home.

I still remember when we were all home to celebrate Christmas. Dad was sitting at the table, and Mom was bringing a goose she had prepared for dinner. Dad reached for the knife to cut the meat, and we all gave thanks to the Lord for everything, and especially for bringing Dad home. When Dad started to cut the goose, I saw blood dripping from his cheek. Everything went very fast. Dad put his hand on his cheek, Mom got some towels, and I helped Dad put pressure on his bleeding cheek. We had to get Dad to the hospital fast. We had no phone, and it was Christmas, so most people were celebrating. I told Mom to keep pressure on the cheek and went with my brother to try to get some help. I ran in the street and waived my arms to stop a car. I told Jesus to help me, and I cried out to the Lord to save my dad.

I saw a car turning and began to run. The driver stopped, and it was our friend from the grocery store. He jumped out of his car and yelled at me but soon recognized me, and he knew that he needed to help Dad. When we brought dad to the car, I was afraid I would never see him again because he was very pale, and his lips were blue. I tried to check his pulse on the way to the car. Mom went with Dad, and Tom, the owner from the grocery store, told me he would come back, pick us up, and take us to the hospital to be with Dad on Christmas.

It was very quiet, and I still remember Mom when we came to the hospital. She was crying. We thought Dad was gone and it was too much for her. I tried to talk to Mom and told her that God was in charge and we had to trust Him.

Mom looked at me and said that God had saved Dad and he was okay. One of the radiation treatments had caused the bleeding because a piece of the radium needle was left in, and if he hadn't gone to the hospital he would have died because he would have bled to death.

Before Dad came back from the operating room, we all went to the chapel, and on our knees we gave thanks to the Lord because it was only the Lord who had saved my dad. He had given us every help. Tom was also sure that this was a miracle and that the Lord made him drive this way instead of the usual way he drove almost every day. Somehow on Christmas Day he turned on the wrong street and didn't know why he did it, until he saw me in the middle of the road. Tom was not a person who was very close to the Lord. He always believed when things were unusual that there was a logical explanation. He did not agree when people used the word "miracle." I was very surprised when Tom told the doctor that the Lord indeed taught him a lesson, and he would never question any unusual event and healing.

Yes, the Lord changed Tom, and everyone who knew the old Tom could see it because he became very kind and helped families who didn't have enough to pay for their food. He started a special program, and twice a month he offered free food to needy families. But this was not the only thing he did. He always told everyone that it was all in the Lord's hands, and we should never doubt the Lord. When people said, "But, Tom, where is your explanation?" Tom smiled and answered, "God is the only explanation for anything that happens in our life!"

Trust in the Lord and do not ask Him why, where, or when. He is the only one who has all the answers. God is the one who gives us life and will call us when our journey on this earth ends.

I had to stop for a while and will now try to bring my words in another direction because I will soon finish my writing. If it is in the Lord's plan, I will try to publish it, and it will be my testimony for my family, friends, and everyone who reads my words. I know in my heart that there is a reason for me to write this book. There are also moments sometimes when I have the desire to stop because the next chapters in my journey are not easy to tell, and I need the Lord to guide me in the right direction. I think He is the only one who can bring the right words into my heart and mind, so I will pray and ask the Lord to help me because I have a very difficult time to write without hesitation.

I have said before that my dad committed suicide and my mom died 1995, in Germany. One year later, my husband died after being sick for over a year with prostate cancer. I had to take care of everything and tried to make enough to pay all the bills, but I had to get help from my son Daniel and had to make the decision to leave Warroad after twenty-three years and move to Thief River Falls to work at a motel as a night clerk. Since I had worked in other motels, it was not very difficult for me to do the job, and besides, the owner of the motel was a strong believer in the Lord and helped me to understand and master things the easy way. To this day we are still in touch, and Don and Cheri are wonderful friends and a special blessing in my life. I can call Cheri anytime, and I will always get the right answer. I have to say if we let God bring the right friends into our lives we will be blessed forever. We can only look at people's faces, but God sees people's hearts, and if we follow the Lord and trust Him, we will never fail.

22

Learning to Control Anger and Make Others Smile

When I moved away from Warroad, I thought this would be the last time for me to pack all my belongings and start new in another town. I made new friends and had to get used to living in an apartment home. It was much smaller, and we had to get rid of many items. I had no problems doing my job and went twice during my time to pool school to become a certified pool operator. I also worked on the front desk. Soon I saw again that the Lord was in charge of my life, and the first sign came shortly after I lived in Thief River Falls. It was when He sent me to the Holy Land, and Don and Cheri where very happy that I had the chance to see Israel and to walk where our Lord Jesus had walked when He was on this earth. I also was in charge of taking care of the decorations in the motel for all the seasons, especially for Christmas. It was a special treat for me, and I still love to do that.

It makes a big difference for the whole atmosphere in our lives when we start to decorate our home. I know when I was a child my mom always decorated our home with flowers and handmade things like embroidered pillows or table cloths, and it was very special. Mom taught me to do embroidery, knitting, and crocheting, and to this day I still knit and crochet. I also passed it on to my daughter, and not long ago, I helped three of my granddaughters learn the techniques of knitting and crocheting. Every time I go to visit, my grandchildren are eager to show me their newest project, and I feel the touch of my mom when she was teaching me and I brought her my project. I also remember when she corrected me, and I had to do it over again. I was not very happy, but I learned when you make a mistake, face it and do not cover it up, because it will get worse, and by the end you will undo it and start over again. I can't remember how many things I knit and crocheted, but I know that I knit and crocheted for my children, and I also made many blankets and pillow cases for friends and neighbors. It is always special when we make things and work on it, because anyone can go to a store and buy a present, but not everyone can crochet, sew, or knit. A simple homemade project has more value than an expensive store item because it is made with love and will be treasured forever.

My mom had a box, and she kept every picture and every writing from my brothers and me, and no one was allowed to throw any paper away. When I left Germany, Mom opened the box, and with tears in her eyes she said, "When I feel lonely, I will look at all the pictures you have drawn over the years, and I will read all the words you wrote, and I can go on because you are not far away. Alusru, you are very special, my child, and you will be forever in my heart."

When I left, I didn't exactly understand the meaning, but when I was far away, I began to realize why Mom kept all the things from us and treasured every picture we drew and every word we wrote. When I became a mom, I did the same, and I still have many things from my children I will treasure. Now I have my own treasure box and fill it with words and pictures from my grandchildren. To tell you the truth, I do believe that every mom treasures drawings and writings from her children. All year long I always had all kinds of pictures on my wall and used magnets to put things up on my refrigerator and stove. Nothing is more precious than the first picture your child makes for Mom or Dad, even if it is only scribble, and no one can see what it is. Only your child can tell you what he or she had drawn. It was drawn with love and only meant to be given to Mom or Dad.

My children had special things they drew when they got a little older. Ricky always used every color and told me it was Jesus. Chris was very good and drew houses with every detail, and the most important part was to put on the roof antenna so the kids could watch TV. Michael liked bugs, spiders, and guns, and Daniel loved to make pictures with cars and tractors. Pam always put flowers with the sun and many stars on her first pictures. I have to say it was indeed very special, and when I look back now I can see why each one had different interests.

Ricky loved Jesus and went to be with the Lord. When he used the beautiful colors, he told me he needed them to make windows and the rainbow for Jesus. From the very start, Chris was interested in detailed pictures, and he drew many special pictures with nature's beauty. Later he drew people and cartoon characters. Michael still loves snakes and bugs, and Daniel was only six when he went behind the wheel. To this day he is still interested in all kinds of cars. Pam loves flowers and plants, and today she uses beautiful cards and pictures on her computer to tell the world how much she loves God's creation. Since she thinks she can't draw, she uses wonderful words to share with everyone.

When I look at my grandchildren, I can also see when they got a little older that the girls had almost the same interests their mom had. The boys didn't like words, and so both boys love to draw. Manny is the oldest boy and had many problems when he started school, but he could draw any picture. I also could see that he used his drawings to master other small problems. To say a final word about my children and all my wonderful grandchildren, I have to say that the Lord has touched everyone and given all of them different gifts. It is up to each one how to use it.

Sometimes we need to close our eyes and not say a word when children make a wrong decision or want to do things their way. But if we pray and ask the Lord to watch and guide our children, they will soon feel God's gentle touch and turn around. Prayers are more powerful than anything else. Over the years I have learned that a conversation with God is sometimes the only answer to solve a problem. God will give you His answer, and it is up to you to follow Him. I also know sometimes we think we have all the answers, and we should do it the easy way and listen to others, but when we get in deep trouble and ignore God's advice, we are still able to call on Him;

He will pull us back with His unconditional love. We don't have to be worried anymore. God is never far, and we can reach Him anytime during our time here on Earth. All we have to do is listen to the Lord and trust Him. If we do what God tells us to do, we will be amazed how fast all our doubts disappear.

God likes to see us happy, and I think that is the reason He created the beauty of this world with flowers, stars, and sunshine. He created every animal and every tree with a simple command of His voice: "Let there be light!" First came the light, and God called it Day, and the darkness He called Night. This was God's first day of His creation. On the second day, God divided the waters and He created the sky and called it Heaven. Then God gathered the waters under the sky and created the dry land. He called the waters Oceans and Sea, and the dry land He called Earth, and God filled the earth with flowers, grass, trees, and fruit. Every plant had its own seed to prosper and multiply, and this was the third day. On the fourth day, God made two lights and placed both in the sky to light up the earth. The big light was the sun to shine during the day, and the smaller light was the moon with all the stars to guide the night. On the fifth day, God filled the sky with birds, butterflies, bees, and bugs, and the sea and ocean He filled with big and small fishes and sea creatures. God was very satisfied with His work, and on the sixth day created all the animals of the earth and also the first man. God created everything in six days. On the seventh day, God rested and He blessed that day and called the day holy.

God created everything, but His greatest creation was man because He formed man from the dust of the earth, and blew into man the breath of life. God gave him a beautiful garden to live in. In the middle of the garden, God planted two trees; one was the tree of life, and the other was the tree of knowledge. When God decided to give man a comparable helper, He took a rib from man, made a woman, and gave the woman to the man. The man he called Adam, and Adam called the woman Eve.

God was very happy and satisfied with all of His wonderful creation, and He told Adam that every plant and tree would have fruit to eat; only one tree was not to be eaten, and this was the tree of knowledge of good and evil. God told Adam if he ate the fruit he would surely die. But when the snake in the tree told Eve it was because He didn't want them to be like God Himself, Eve took the beautiful-looking fruit and ate it, and she also convinced Adam to eat it.

Soon both found out they were naked, and when God called Adam, he and his wife Eve hid themselves from the presence of the Lord because they became afraid. God knew that Adam and Eve had ignored His warning and took the fruit from the tree of knowledge. There were so many trees they could eat from, but they chose the tree God had told them not to touch. God was disappointed and angry because Adam blamed Eve, Eve blamed the snake, God cursed all, and to this day man has to work all his life to have enough food and shelter for his children, and the woman has great pain to bring forth children. The snake was cursed to crawl on its belly and to eat dust.

God had given man everything, and man could be living happily without any worries if he would have obeyed God's command. This was the first sin, and it changed everything. To this day people haven't changed because they want to be better than others, and many will do whatever it takes to get what they want regardless of what or if it is right or wrong, if it is the truth or a lie. When people didn't listen to God and the whole world was full of sin, God was ready to destroy everything; however, one man was not a sinner, so God saved Noah, his family, the animals, and other living creatures. The sinners and all the other things, God destroyed with a flood. He was angry and very disappointed in the world, but He gave us another chance to change. God also promised not to destroy the earth again, and He put a beautiful rainbow into the sky to mark His promise.

But the world did not change. God gave people a second chance, and when the Lord sacrificed His own Son Jesus Christ, many people didn't believe that He was the Son of God, even though they witnessed the miracle here on Earth. Jesus healed people, but most didn't believe He was the Messiah who came to save the world, so they crucified the son of God. God was again disappointed and angry, but Jesus called out to His father, "Father, forgive them because they don't know what they are doing!"

God didn't destroy the world and kill every human. Instead, another miracle was given to this world. The tomb where the body of Jesus was put to rest after He was tortured and crucified was empty, and God lifted His son back to His Kingdom in Heaven. Yes, my Jesus is alive and risen from the dead.

How long will it be before the world believes God is the only one who is in charge of life and death, and that people have no power to change it? Why can't people understand that God is the creator of Heaven and Earth? I know science is wonderful, and it is great to learn things, but I think scientists should tell the truth and let the world know that God is the beginning and the end of every life. If man was able to stop tragedies or death with a simple command of his voice, he would be almost like God, but no human can command a storm or a roaring ocean to stop. We all know that no scientist can stop thunder and lightning with devastating heavy rainfall. Man can predict the weather but has no power to stop it. When a heavy storm hits the earth during the daytime, after the storm is over, most of the time we can see God's hand because a beautiful rainbow appears in the sky. It is God's promise that He will be watching over the world; all we have to do is believe and trust.

God is only a prayer away and will give everyone who believes and calls out to Him His unconditional love. We don't need to wait. We do not have to pay. It doesn't matter if we are poor or rich, black or white, old or young, God will be there because Jesus Christ paid for all our sins with the cross and His blood, and Jesus Christ is the answer for this world. Satan loses when people call on Jesus Christ!

I think this is the reason for all the things happening in the world. Some people absolutely refuse to believe in God, and sometimes they worship and glorify Satan because he promised them power and abundant wealth, just like the snake promised Eve she would become like God. People reach out for power and will do whatever Satan whispers and orders them to do. It doesn't make any difference what price they have to pay. Satan will promise anything—like if they follow him they will become rich and famous. This is a highly effective weapon Satan uses to get people under his spell. Satan will also try to get people when they reach out to drugs and alcohol. When we walk away from the Lord and follow Satan, sure, we might become rich and famous and have power, but Satan will rule our life, and he will not be satisfied until he has destroyed another life. Sometimes it will end up in murder or suicide. It is a fact that when people are rich and have power, they will do anything to keep it and to gain more. This is Satan, and he has no mercy.

Jesus Christ is the Savior and the only answer because He gave His life to save us. If we pray, obey, and love one another, He will help us go anywhere and will give us comfort and peace. We have to make the decision to follow Christ and He will protect us if our faith comes under the attack of Satan. All we have to do is put our faith in Jesus Christ. We must turn away from sin and Satan's promises and surrender to our Lord Jesus Christ. We will be amazed with His love and holiness, with His passion and challenge. Only Jesus Christ can challenge us with truth and amaze us with God.

I can't understand why it is so difficult to follow the Lord and to lean on Him. Is it so hard to live by His word and commandments? Love one another, love they neighbor, love they enemy! Give instead of receive. Try to forgive someone. Be satisfied, and if you have enough try to help others. Always remember when your time is over, it doesn't matter how much money, gold, silver, or other earthly things you have in your possession. You have to leave it all, because you can't take it with you. You can't make a deal when you die; it is over, it is done, and all your beauty and millions are gone.

Your life is worthless if you only listen to Satan, because he is a liar and thief, and he doesn't care about you. He will laugh, and if you suffer, he will be happy and you will not be able to change it. But if you followed the Lord, you will have peace. God never leaves you, and He will comfort you when you call Him because He loves you and gives you strength. Over the years I have learned that people will disappoint you regardless who they are. Sometimes it is your own family, and sometimes it is a stranger who will amaze you with unbelievable words. I have learned to look for people who love to share about the Lord, and also for people who need the Lord. I always ask the Lord to bring people to me. When I am upset, disappointed, frustrated, and angry, I know it is time for me to give it all to the Lord and take time out from the world. I call Jesus, and I can feel He is holding me and comforting me. He gives me all the strength and courage I need to go on with my life and to hold on to the Lord.

I am not perfect, and I never will be without sin because I still live on this earth. The world is full of liars and sinners, and I am human. Sometimes it is much easier to get angry, to yell, to walk away from the Lord, and to follow the crowd and the sinners. After all, who cares if I lose control? I am just human, and it feels good to let the world know that I will not be treated unfairly. But the reality is that Satan got a hold of me, I began to listen to him, and step by step I followed Satan because it was so easy. After all, I needed that. I thought I had no other choice and let the steam out. Instead, I could have avoided all the pain the world put me in and given it to Jesus.

When I finally realized it was not the right answer to get angry, I felt empty and helpless. I called the Lord to help me, and it was so easy because I didn't need to make an appointment or pay a fee. God was right there. He was only a prayer away, and I felt His love right at the moment I called. I think if I had walked away from the Lord and followed the advice from people, I would be lonely and miserable. I would not be able to go on with my life. I also wouldn't be able to share the Lord.

For me it is a reward to have the opportunity to tell others how wonderful and great God is. I have to say that my grandfather Opa fulfilled his duty and calling to tell me all about Jesus Christ. Sometimes I have the feeling that Opa is still pushing me in the right direction, and when I am angry and frustrated, I think about his understanding and kindness. I call on the Lord because that was exactly what Opa did. I think today that God brings special people in our lives, and Opa was very special. Every time I had to face a problem, I heard Opa telling me what to do. When I was a child in similar situations, he pointed his finger to the Lord and asked me, "What do you think what Jesus would do?"

I know there are so many moments where I could get very angry and want to walk away from all the problems, but somehow I cannot. Instead, I have to talk to the Lord, and I am able to do it without anyone stopping or interrupting me because I am all alone in my car driving to my work, or coming home from my work.

Yes, I am still working, and I love it because I can share the Lord! I can tell everyone how wonderful He is and that is the most important reason for me to work. The Lord told me to work.

23

Getting Remarried and a Special Trip to Texas

As I come to the end of my story, it is not easy for me to write it. In 2009, I had the desire to find another man who was alone and close to the Lord. I wanted a man to share the rest of my life with, and I started to try to find him the same way I had found my first husband, Dennis. I signed up with eHarmony, and after several months I switched to Match.com. I received several requests, but most were in other states, and I did not want to make any commitment without first meeting him.

I could not believe that I would love a man I had never met, but I knew that the Lord had answered my prayers. I dreamed about my new love. One day I wrote a poem and asked a question: How can it be? How can it be that you love me when you never saw my face, when you never kissed me? How can it be? It only can be by God's wonderful grace because God knows you and me! How can it be that I love you when I have never seen you and never touched your face? It can only be by God's grace because He touched you and me!

It took until the end of 2010 for me to finally make the decision to meet Jerry. He also lived in Minnesota, and his profile and picture were very good. He was three years older and told me he was a retired pilot living alone, and that he definitely loved the Lord. He was married but his wife had died. He said he had no children, and he was very much interested in meeting me.

I agreed to drive halfway from Thief River to meet with Jerry at a restaurant. I remember when I saw him I was very nervous. After several times meeting at the same place, we became closer and I fell in love with him. I knew I wanted to marry him as soon as possible because I wanted to become his wife. I knew I could never replace his first wife who had died, but I wanted to give him all my love to make it easier for him. After all, I had also lost my soul mate. He was my love for over twenty-six years and the father of my wonderful children. I knew it was not easy, but I wanted to fill my life again with a new love, and I was willing to do anything to make it possible.

We met as often as possible, and after Jerry met my children and purchased a beautiful ring, we got engaged on Valentine's Day in 2011, and made plans to set a wedding date. Many times Jerry sent beautiful roses to my workplace in Thief River. We made all kinds of plans because we wanted to have our own home and do whatever we wanted to do.

We decided to purchase a home, and I went with Jerry to many places to find the right one—to enjoy and to make it our own. I was very happy and looked forward to marrying Jerry. My children helped me make plans for the big day. Trista went with me to pick out a beautiful dress; it was black and white—a very elegant, long dress.

The date was set, and Don and Cheri helped me arrange and plan for May 7, 2011. I asked the Lord to give me words for my vows. I wanted to say them in the church. This is what the Lord gave me:

True love! God gives us answers when we pray. God gives us miracles each day. When two hearts fall in love, this is a great miracle from above. True love is precious, not for sale. True love forgives and will not fail. True love never ages, nor does it grow old. True love is warm and sweet, not bitter or cold. True love is kind, without guilt or expectation. True love is gratitude and consideration. True love is God's voice to trust and obey. True love teaches to be still, to pause, and to pray! Let your life be joy and true love! Let us honor the Lord and His gift from above! Let us walk with Jesus side by side. May God bless our marriage and be our guide! May God bless this holy wedding day! May God bless all of you today! This is my prayer, I pray!

I wanted to say all these words to Jerry out loud in front of everyone who came to the church, but I was glad I wrote all the words down, because when I walked down to the altar, I forgot everything. I couldn't remember the words I had written, and so I had to read them.

I remember I was very nervous, and when I got ready to put the beautiful wedding dress on, I needed the help of Trista my daughter-in-law because the dress did not fit. I had lost some weight, and the dress was shoulder free. Trista took my Jesus pin and pulled it together to hold the dress up. Also, I felt like walking on a high floor that was moving because I had never walked in shoes with very high heels. For my wedding, my shoes had very high heels.

My son Daniel walked me to the altar and was holding me because he could see that I was walking like an elephant in a glass store (we would say this in Germany) I finally made it, and Jerry was waiting for me. My daughter Pamela sang in German, "*So Nimm Denn Meine Haende*" ("Oh Take My Hands Dear Father"), and my first granddaughter Katie sang "How Great Thou Art." Pastor Joe gave a wonderful message, and after the ceremony and lighting two candles, he announced that Jerry and I were husband and wife. We had a very nice wedding, and the church was filled with all of my friends and family.

Jerry had only one brother and his wife. He told me that he had another brother but he was sick, and his daughter lived in Texas. He also told me he had a son, but he could not get along with his son's wife, so he had no contact with his son for years.

I didn't question anything. When I said something, Jerry became very upset, and I thought it probably was too painful for him to talk about. When I tried to ask him about his wife who had passed away, he told me not to ask. I always thought he still missed her, and I knew it was not easy to talk about someone you loved, to whom you were married, and who was now gone.

After we got married, we looked for a house. By the end of 2011, we moved to Little Falls in a nice house we had purchased after many visits to different homes up for sale. Jerry had met my family, and he had no problem when I told him that I needed to have a home where I could have my son Chris and my little dog Toby living with us because I was Chris's guardian, and Toby was my dog when we still lived in Warroad. When we looked at the house in Little Falls, it was perfect for all; Chris would have two nice rooms downstairs and Toby could stay with him during the night. During the day, he was on the deck or he had freedom to run in a fenced area. It was perfect (I thought).

I never paid much attention to some changes in my husband and his reaction to simple things. When we went shopping one day, I had the first fight with him over a $5.00 purchase I had made. It was a little purse, and it was on sale. Jerry got mad and told me if I bought it I would have to walk home because he would leave. First, I thought he was just kidding, so I told him, "You are the one who will walk because I have the keys to my car."

Jerry left and I purchased the purse. When I went to my car, Jerry came and tried to give me a lecture to listen to him when he tells me not to buy things. I was very stunned. What was his problem? I was paying for everything, and he had no right to act out like he did. After all, I was his wife not a child. What was wrong with him? I soon found out when he told me, "You are *my* wife, and you do what I tell you to do. When I make a decision, you don't need to question me."

I was very much hurt. What was wrong? This was not the same Jerry. Where were his kindness and his understanding? Where were his promises and concern? I had to get his permission to do things because he made all the decisions. In other words, he was the commander in chief, and Chris, Toby, and I were the little soldiers standing up, shouting, *Yes, sir!* or *No, sir!* I thought it would eventually change, and since Jerry was very busy with his daily stock market business during the week, I began making the house more like a home.

One weekend we went to visit Jerry's brother and sister-in-law, and I also met his other brother and sister-in-law. I really believed things might change and we would have a better understanding to solve problems and difficulties. I thought my husband would see how wonderful it is to have a marriage built with love, respect, and harmony. But nothing would change, and when I tried to get away from all the fighting and yelling, I went to listen to my Christian music. I locked my door and ignored my husband's order to turn the music off and unlock the door. We got into a heated argument, and Jerry ordered Chris to call the police. I could not believe my husband went that far to get his way.

Soon I made the decision to start working again. I filled out many applications and could not find a job in Little Falls. I talked to my son in Alex, and he called me one day and told me that a new hotel in Alex was looking for a night clerk. At first I thought it was probably very unlikely they would hire me because of my age, but I decided to give it a try and go to the interview. I was hired and received a call shortly after the interview. My family and friends could not believe I wanted to work again.

I tried many things to bring change into the painful situation in our oh-so-short marriage. We went to church, and I made arrangements to ask a Christian counselor for advice to have a happy marriage, but after several sessions, Jerry refused to participate. I went to work at the hotel in Alex, and at first I stayed at Daniel's house. Later I stayed at Michael's place because it was not a good idea to drive every day.

I really liked my work, and I had to learn many things. It wasn't easy because most of the night audit information, and all of the reservations, were documented on the computer. I didn't like the computer, but step by step, I lost the fear I had for any computer. Sometimes I still get very frustrated because I hit the wrong key or can't find the right answer, and sometimes I am afraid that the guest won't want to wait for me to type all the information. I am definitely not a professional person when it comes to typing, but I have a powerful weapon I wear on my uniform beside my name tag—a special pin that says "I Love Jesus." When things are difficult, I put my hand over the pin and ask the Lord to help me. Nothing—absolutely nothing—is impossible for God. If He is for me, no one can be against me! I also have to say, *Lord, not my will, Your will be done. Amen!* This is the only answer to all problems, and God never makes a mistake.

Before I started working the night shift at the Alex hotel in August of 2012, I asked the Lord to help me. He did and still does. I also asked the Lord to tell me what I could do for Him. The answer is always the same: *Trust Me, love Me, and spread My name!*

Well, at first I talked to the guests when they checked in. Some needed to tell me they really liked my Jesus pin. I shared some reasons why I was wearing the pin, and after a while I knew what I needed to do. I had to help people lean on the Lord, to trust Him with all their hearts, and to give it all to Him. I took my pin and gave it to the guests before they went to their rooms. I told the guests I needed to do it and that the Lord wants us to tell the world we love Jesus!

Sometimes we can't understand when the Lord gives us a sign or opens a door, but if we do exactly what He tells us to do, we will be surprised of the outcome. I am very thankful that I can still work and have the golden opportunity to talk to guests and share the Lord with the people.

I was working at the hotel for over a year, and Jerry made the decision to visit his daughter in Texas. At first I thought to let him go alone, but then I decided to talk to my manager and ask for some days off. I was a little nervous to meet Jerry's daughter, her husband, and her son, because every time Jerry and I had an argument, he told me that if Brenda met me she would not be very pleased with me. I wasn't sure if I could be in her life because she had lost her mom, and now her dad was married to another woman.

I prayed and asked the Lord. I didn't really get a yes or no from the Lord, and I had the feeling that the answer was *you decide, My child*. Jerry had a beautiful picture from his daughter, and before I gave Jerry my answer, I looked at Brenda's picture and saw her smile.

She was holding her son, and at that moment I knew I had to fly with Jerry to Texas.

We booked the tickets, packed our suitcases, and flew to Dallas, Texas. Finally, after some delays and a long wait time, we landed in Dallas. Jerry spotted his son-in-law, and a very tall, handsome young man gave me a big hug. I will never ever forget that moment when this young man said, "Welcome to Texas! Can I call you Oma?"

At that moment, I knew I had gained a wonderful grandson and that he was close to the Lord. I felt very much honored by his request. When Brenda gave me a hug, I connected with her right away. I knew I could never take her mom's place, but I could try to be a good friend and help her to let her mom rest in peace. I didn't want to talk to her about her mom, and I knew that time would close and heal wounds, so I decided just to tell her that I would pray for her—that God would surround her with His unconditional love and grace.

We had a very nice time, and the only problems we had were Jerry and the stock market. Brenda was not very happy that her dad was spending time on the computer to watch the up and downs of the stock market. We went to many places and had a great time. Every day I felt more and more welcomed. I enjoyed every day, and even though I am not a sports fan, I went to watch my special new grandson playing baseball. Brenda did everything to give us a wonderful time. We both went to the old Texas stores, and I bought souvenirs for my family in Minnesota. I had a difficult time saying goodbye, and I wished we stayed longer. Brenda became a close friend, Aaron was such a wonderful young man, and Chris was very friendly and had no problem repeating a question for me when I didn't understand. At this time I didn't know I had lost 78% of my hearing.

We left Texas and flew back to Minnesota. I promised Brenda to stay in touch with her, and email and call whenever I had a chance. I shared many things with my "new" daughter and purchased some little things for her because I wanted to see her happy. It was soon Christmas, and I went to all my catalogs to find some unique gifts. I had no problems ordering all the things, and it was a special reward for me to pack a Christmas package with love and special messages to Brenda, Chris, and Aaron.

When I talked with Brenda, I told her that I just love Christmas and that it was a time to love and care about others. I also told her that it was very difficult at first for me to celebrate Christmas after Ricky passed away because it happened just before Christmas. Brenda told me that she also loved Christmas, and it was also not easy to celebrate because just a year ago, on December 25, 2011, her mom had died.

At first, I thought I misunderstood, so I asked, "Brenda, did you say your mom passed away last year in December?"

Brenda said yes and that that year was the first year without Mom; she was sick for a long time.

I needed to get off the phone. I felt like I had been hit by a ton of bricks. I was unable to say much and found a lame excuse to hang up the phone. I don't know how long it took me to breathe normally and to calm down. Jerry and I got married in May 2011. Jerry told me that his wife had passed away when we met. I pulled the papers I had from match.com and read every word: *I am a Christian and a widower....*Here it was, *a widower*! Why did he say that his wife had passed away? We got married in May of 2011, and he never told me that his wife, Brenda's mom, was still alive. He didn't tell me the truth, and I was very much hurt.

When I asked him, he told me it wasn't my business, and she left him for another guy. I had to put a question mark on his statement— was it really true? If Brenda hadn't told me that her mom had passed away a year ago, Jerry probably never would have told me.

Brenda and I became very close, and I shared with her many things. My new daughter also sent me a beautiful glass ornament, and it was very special because I loved the bright colors. I hung it up close to my bed and window. I started to pull out the decorations for the Christmas tree and decided to put the tree up because I had to work on Christmas, and it was always a treat for me to decorate our tree each year with all kinds of special decorations. Each year I also decorated my home with candles in the windows and the manger from Israel under the tree. I didn't know that all this would change. Jerry had no intention of letting me do all those special things because it cost more for electricity to have a tree with color-changing lights and to have the lights on all day.

This was one of the main reasons for me to volunteer to work on Christmas. I absolutely love Christmas, and I love candles and the smell of fir and cone. During Christmastime we have the lights on all day and night, and I did the same when I lived in Warroad and Thief River. So what if it cost a few dollars more? Christmas is special!

Well, now I was married to Jerry, and he didn't like it when I turned the tree lights on during the day, and every answer was *turn the lights off; it costs too much money.* I bought fiber-optic candles and ornaments with glitter and sounds, but all of it was powered by batteries. Still I had to turn off the candles when he went to bed because my husband needed to have it pitch dark—no more talking, and definitely no music. Oh boy, what a change for me! I decided to wear earphones to listen to my music and the TV in the living room when I was home. Was it really a *home*? My son didn't dare talk to me because Jerry would get furious when he heard a voice.

I felt like I was a stranger in my own house just being accepted. I started to overlook many things. I had to wear hearing aids to be able to understand people talking to me, but I had no problem to do my work. I also had a powerful weapon against my husband and his demanding behavior. All I needed to do to have a peaceful time at my home was turn off the hearing aids. I was getting tired of all the insults and orders. I also knew this was not an answer to a better relationship because it was tearing us apart, and soon we would have no communication.

I asked the Lord in all my prayers and was ready to walk away from the marriage, when I received a call from my son telling me Jerry was in much pain and was very sick. I went home, and I asked the Lord to give my husband more time. I made a promise to the Lord that I would do anything He wanted me to do. If He wanted me to be with Jerry and not leave him I would do it. It wouldn't be easy for me to walk away from everything. The Lord gave me His answer, and He took away the pain and suffering. Jerry received several treatments and medications, and his problems were under control.

I thought things would change and Jerry would be more of a husband and companion, but as soon as he was feeling better, he went back to his old habits and made life miserable for everyone. My family and friends urged me to put an end to it, but the Lord had answered my prayer when Jerry was sick, and I had to keep my promise.

I am married to Jerry, and I am his wife till death do us part. The Lord will never do things without a reason, and He knows the answer to any question. He is the only one who knows when our time on Earth is running out and the life clock will stop ticking. Nothing will change it, and everyone has to die. No money, no power, no crying, no fighting, no deals, no fame, can change our end. We are all in the same boat—the rich, the poor, the famous, the old, the young, and the beautiful. Nothing can stop death. No one knows the hour, the month, the year, or the date when it will be over and the heart will stop beating.

I will now come to the last pages of my book. When God gives us His answers to our prayers, we should never question Him! God never makes a mistake! Every day I feel I'm coming closer and closer to the Lord, but I also know that Satan is trying very hard to stop me, and I think he is using my marriage, my friends, and my family, but he is also trying to use my work, my health, and my problems. When I started to write my life chapters on a word processor twenty or more years ago, I had no idea that everything would be lost after I had already written over two hundred fifty pages, and that I would start again twenty years later on a computer.

I never will be an expert in writing and using a computer to document everything. Typing my whole life story and saving it all day after day on the computer was a whole new world for me, and I am still a little afraid that if I don't have every word on paper it will be lost someday. I will make sure I soon get to the end so I am able to print it all out and finish the book. What if one day the computer breaks down and I can't find the pages? I am afraid that the pages and all my typing will be gone.

I learned to communicate and to write by using a pen and paper only; I was never taught typing with ten fingers. When my kids see me typing with two fingers, they laugh, but I say, at least I get it done. This is my way to try new things and also not to give up right away. I remember many times when my mom said to me, "The word 'can't' is not in my dictionary; you need to find the word 'try'!"

Sometimes I was amazed how easy the assignment was. I did the same with my children and told them all to never give up before giving it a try. But there are moments when all our answers are wrong, and we get frustrated because we can't find the right answer. We need to stop, pause, and pray, because God is only a prayer away. Soon all our problems are melted away. I do believe it often takes a long time before we finally ask God for help. I had to ask the Lord to help me remember and write each day, to find the right words and also the right time to write. I never thought I would be able to share my life story with anyone, but over the years I've learned that this was what the Lord wanted me to do.

24

God Brings a Special Reporter into My Life

Now I have come to the end of the story, and I want to embrace all of my friends and family. Believe me, you all mean so much to me, and you all deserve to be remembered in my pages. When I ask myself who the number one person in my life was to put me in the right direction, I will always answer, Opa; he told me about Jesus, and he planted the desire in my heart to follow the Lord. Trust the Lord and obey Him. Follow His command, and spread His love to the ones who need Him.

Sometimes I can't understand why people would rather gamble with their lives instead of seeking God's answers. Many times I fell down deep, and God picked me up and put me back on my right road.

Satan has tried many times to change my heart, and often he almost succeeded. I've said many times over that God will answer our prayer, but often we don't like His answer. So when we pray, we need to close our prayer with, *not my will, Your will be done*. We need to give it *all* to the Lord. He will reward us with His unconditional love. He will give us people who want to be in our lives and people who need the Lord in theirs.

When I was told I would never be able to have any children, I accepted it for a while, but then I asked the Lord and He rewarded me with a good husband, Dennis, who was always good to me. We were married twenty-six years and had five children. We had our ups and downs, but I know Dennis really loved me and tried very hard to do whatever he could, and I know he believed in the Lord.

Yes, every child is a gift and a reward from the Lord. I am thankful for all my children, and each one has a special place in my heart. I thank the Lord for blessing my daughter Pamela with Troy—

her caring and believing husband, and father to all her children. Pamela and Troy both love the Lord. They built a wonderful foundation for the children, and each one learned very early, *Jesus loves me.*

Katie and Jessica are my first grandchildren, and I love both very much. Both girls are now on their own journeys, and I know both girls love the Lord. Emanuel is my first grandson, and I know he is always seeking the Lord because he loves Jesus. Jacob was the little one for a long time until God blessed the family with another wonderful new arrival. Jacob is also close to the Lord, and he knows that Jesus loves him. Ariel is the sunshine in the family, and I know that she loves Jesus. Pamela will always love the Lord with all her heart, and Troy is standing with her. Both are teaching and guiding the children in God's way, and I am very thankful to the Lord.

I can also say there were many times for my daughter and her husband to walk away from the Lord because Satan tried to destroy their life, and the family had to pray often for help to provide for the family. God answered in His way. Help came from friends and family, and to this day I know God will always answer—but in His time, often when we don't expect it. I know Troy loves my daughter, and he is trying very hard to make enough to put food on the table, pay the bills, and have a home to live in.

Katie and Jessie are on their own, and Katie is engaged to Jacob, a nice young man. Jessie is also engaged. Kyle and she have a sweet little girl and live in Baudette. Kyle and Jessie are very happy, and their little girl was born last year in November. Her name is Karrah Rhianna.

When Karrah was born, Pam became a grandmother, and I became a great-grandmom. I will not write very much about Katie and Jessie because I think in the near future Jessie will write her own life story, because she also writes poetry. I will say, I have a special love for both of my granddaughters because I was there when Katie entered this world, and I held her in my arms. I was there when she choked on her toy doll, and I called out to the Lord to save her.

Jessie was born in Panama, but she has a very special place in my heart. I was there when she fell on the cement floor in a restaurant. She was very strong and pushed against the table and took a tumble to the floor before anyone could stop it. I was there when she started to walk and talk, and I was there when she danced. I was there when she got in trouble and had to be away from her family, and I was there when God took her under His wings and brought Kyle into her life and blessed both with a beautiful baby girl. Thank You, Lord!

My son Daniel left our family nest very early to be on his own, and he found a wonderful lady; she had two sweet little girls. My son fell in love with the lady and started to build a great foundation for a family filled with love and care. Daniel and Trista had their ups and downs, but one thing I have seen over the years is that Trista became more a daughter to me. I am very happy my son found such a wonderful wife. Both are very hard workers and still find time away from the kids and all the pressure to spend a weekend together, falling in love over again and again. They would both do anything for their gorgeous girls.

Abbigayle is the oldest; she loves horses and animals. Abbi is unafraid, and she is very close to Daniel. When I look at her I can see Daniel when he was little because he always did things and often got himself in trouble. Abbi also ignored rules when she was younger, and many times she got herself in trouble also. Today she has become a young and responsible lady, and I do believe that she will follow her dreams and never walk away from the Lord.

Emma is just the opposite of her sister. She also loves animals and takes care of dogs and cats, but she is more fragile. Her favorite activities are dancing and acting. Emma is also very close to Daniel, and when I look at Emma I can see a beautiful little girl who is stepping in the footsteps of her mom and who loves Jesus.

Danielle is the youngest, and her personality is in between. She loves animals and dancing, and she is very adventurous and unafraid; she will try anything to keep up with her two sisters. She loves to be on the computer and to play games, and I also know she loves Jesus. All three girls are very special to me. I see each one as a precious gift from the Lord.

My oldest son Michael is not married, and he had a very difficult time overcoming problems he had to face after a very bad accident during his time in the army. He went with his friend on a motorcycle, and both got into a bad accident where Michael was thrown down a hill. He fell into a place where nobody could see him. Hours later when his friend woke up in the hospital, he asked for Michael, and the army went to search for him. When they found him they didn't believe he would make it, because he had lost much blood and his leg was almost amputated. It was a miracle he was still alive, and today I think the Lord was right there with him, because later when we received a call from the army, I checked the time and it was the same time I had felt the urge to pray for Michael—that he would not need to go overseas to fight for our country. I told the Lord that I gave Him my youngest son, and I begged Him to keep Michael safe.

Well I said before, the Lord answers prayers in His way and time. When we received the call and found out my son's condition, I had to pray again. I also had many friends praying for him. Today Michael has a difficult time walking. He works for the city and is the owner and landlord of an apartment building in the heart of the city. Michael has two renters, and he lives in the building with two cats. He has to work very hard, but the Lord is watching over him.

One of Michael's renters is over eighty. She loves my son and is doing everything to make life easier for him. She is like a guardian angel, making sure that Michael has good food and help when he needs it. Ivy and I became very good friends, and we have always much fun together. Ivy doesn't have to tell you she loves the Lord; when you meet her, you can see and feel it right away. I have to say Thank You, Lord, for this wonderful, lovely lady!

I have told everything about my children, and the last one I need to talk about is my son Chris. It is not easy for me to paint a clear picture of him because he is a very lonely young man and has a difficult time fitting into society. But Chris has come a long way, and step by step he has started to overcome the abuse he suffered by strange people when he was only a little child taken out of our family. He was separated from his mom and dad and his sister and brother. Besides, when he came back his little brother was gone because he died, and painful memories were all that was left.

Chris and Ricky had a special relationship; Ricky was very close to Chris—like a little angel. When he was sick he often cried for Chris and called him Tistan because he couldn't say Christian. To this day, Chris is still very upset when we talk about the past, and he cherishes all the little toys and things Ricky played with.

Chris tried to work and be on his own, but he had so many problems. I hope he will eventually have enough self-confidence to make the step into the working world. I will do whatever I can, and I know the Lord will guide Chris and help him to walk in the right direction. We tried many programs to help Chris, and he went to different trainings but nothing helped; nothing was effective, and he is still not working. He lives with Jerry and me.

Over the years I have learned that I need to pray for Chris and let the Lord guide him in the right direction because He is the only one who can do anything. He is the only one who has the right answers. It is not easy for a mother to see the pain and anger in her child and feel helpless, but I trust the Lord with my son, and I know God will take care of him. Whatever His answer is, I have to accept it and say *not my will, Lord, Your will be done.* Then I feel peace and don't have to be worried. Nothing is impossible for God.

When God brought Jerry into my life, he gave me not only a new husband, He gave me much more. When I went with Jerry to Texas to meet his daughter, her husband, and their only son, I had no idea I had gained a wonderful new daughter and an exceptional grandson. Only a sentence with five simple words began a wonderful connection with a young man. He came to the airport with his dad, gave me a hug and said, "Can I call you Oma?" We connected right away, and immediately I knew Aaron was special. God had given me a new grandson who really loved the Lord. I told him I would be honored if he called me Oma. Aaron and I have a great relationship, and I thank the Lord every day for this wonderful young man, my new grandson.

I also knew I should not be afraid to meet Brenda, Aaron's mom, Jerry's daughter. Maybe she would understand that I didn't want to take her mom's place. I decided to be very careful not to talk about her mom because I knew how I felt when my mom passed away. No other woman can take a mother's place, and I had no intention to do that; all I wanted was to become her friend. During our visit I didn't say much about her mom, and today I am glad I didn't. Brenda and I became very close, and when I found out a year later her mom didn't pass away when Jerry said, I was very hurt because my husband didn't tell me the truth when we got married.

Only the wonderful relationship with Brenda, Chris, and Aaron gave me hope to change the situation in my oh-so-short marriage. Today we have a wonderful mother-daughter relationship. I am her mum; I told her she can always count on me, and I will always call her my new daughter. I had prayed so many times for Brenda, and I do believe that her mom was a very special and beautiful lady. I told Brenda that her mom is happy to know I am helping her and that we became close friends.

I remember when I lost my mom. A year later my husband died, and I felt very lonely. The Lord brought people into my life who helped me to trust Him.

Don and Cheri are two of the special angels in my life. Both are very close to the Lord and became two of my closest friends over the years. I'd like to thank the Lord for every friend.

When I decided to write my life story, I didn't know if I would ever make the decision to share it with others (besides my family), but now I have the desire to publish it and share it with the world. I know God wants me to do it because He gave me a very special person who told me to write a book and to share it with everyone. Last year she came to interview me, and when she left she said that I needed to write a book. Rachel Barduson is a reporter for a special paper, and she inspired me to write.

I did, and now over a year later, I am writing the last page. I want to particularly say thank you to Rachel who encouraged me and believed in me. Also to my family and friends who are happy that I followed my dream to share the work God did in my life, and still does daily. I thank the Lord for all my friends and my wonderful family, and I would like to say to everyone who reads my book that I only wrote it to tell the world this:

Without the Lord, I would not be here today because He was there when I fell down the mountain cliff. He was there when I was in a deep coma. He was there when I cried out to Him as my family was torn apart. He was there when I had to say goodbye to my little baby and tell him to take his wings and fly to Jesus. He was there when I was diagnosed with cancer and spinal meningitis. He was there when I had to start new, give up my home, and move to a small apartment in a strange city. He was there when I prayed, and He answered each prayer in His way. This is why I had to write to tell the world God is only a prayer away. He is there when you call. Give it all to the Lord! All the glory belongs to God. He is the One who wrote this book, and He gave me every word and I say, Lord, not my will, Your will be done. Amen!

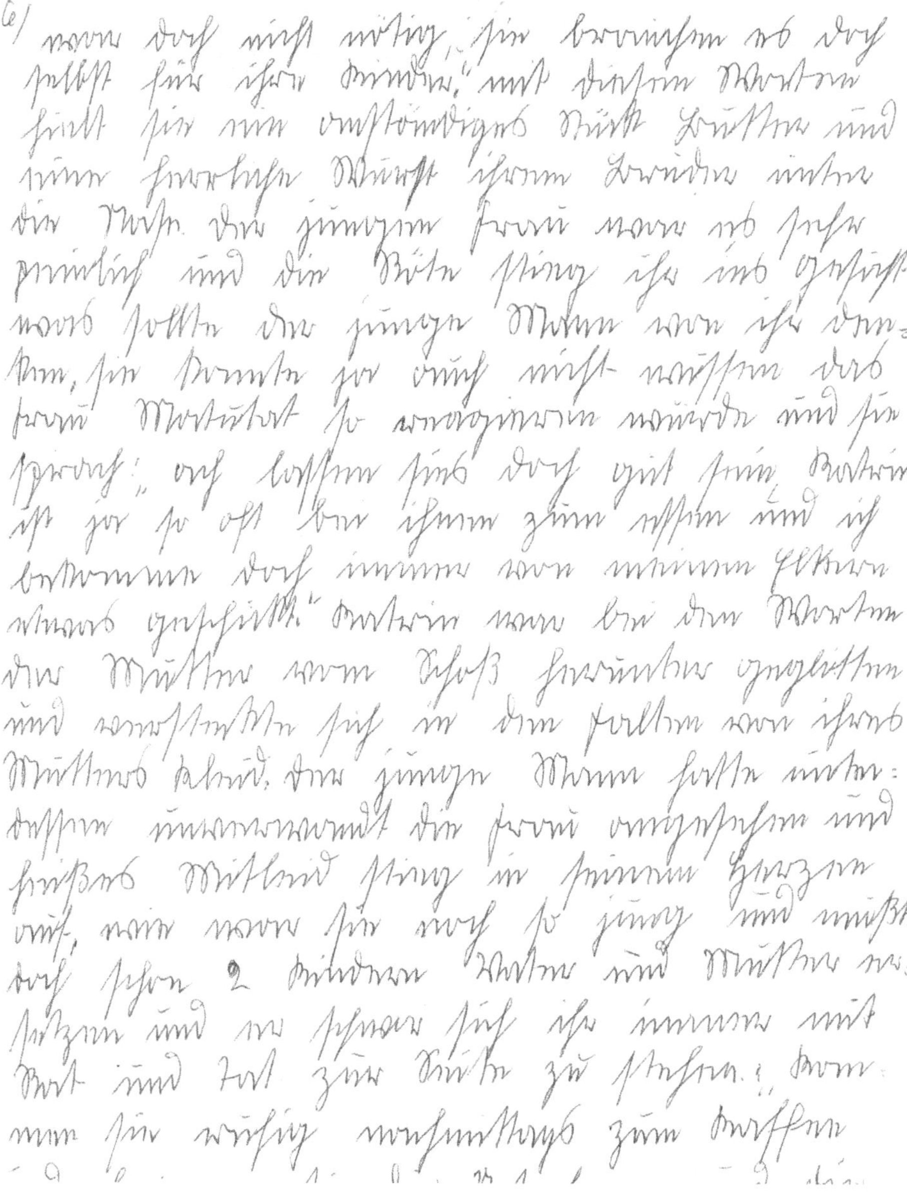
6/ war doch nicht nötig, sie brauchen es doch
selbst für ihre Kinder." mit diesen Worten
hielt sie ein anständiges Stück Butter und
eine herrliche Wurst ihrem Bruder unter
die Nase. Der jungen Frau war es sehr
peinlich und die Röte stieg ihr ins Gesicht.
was sollte der junge Mann von ihr den-
ken, sie konnte ja auch nicht wissen das
seine Mutter so wagemutig würde und sie
sprach: „ach lassen sies doch gut sein, Katrin
ist ja so oft bei ihnen zum essen und ich
bekomme doch immer von meinen Eltern
etwas geschickt." Katrin war bei den Worten
der Mutter vom Schoß herunter geglitten
und versteckte sich in den Falten von ihres
Mutters Kleid. Der junge Mann hatte unter-
dessen unverwandt die Frau angesehen und
heißes Mitleid stieg in seinem Herzen
auf, nein war sie noch so jung und mußte
doch schon 2 Kindern Vater und Mutter er-
setzen und es schwer sich ihr immer mit
Rat und Tat zur Seite zu stehen." Dann
nun sie richtig nachmittags zum Kaffee

Sample of my mother's German handwriting

Sample of my mother's German handwriting

www.ingramcontent.com/pod-product-compliance
Lightning Source LLC
Chambersburg PA
CBHW021051090426
42738CB00006B/283